Ignite Your Leadership

Invite Abundance, Increase Your Income, and Impact the World

A Ladies' Power Lunch Transformation Anthology

Dr. Davia Shepherd & Elizabeth B. Hill, MSW
with Pat Alva-Kraker, Shawniel Chamanlal, LCSW,
Cristal L. Cook, LCSW, Leslie M. Gomez, Teresa Hnat,
Rosemary King, Soribel Martinez, Kelly McCarthy,
Mary Ann Pack, Barb Pritchard, Brittany Quagan, MS, LPC,
Kathleen Troy, Joan Reed Wilson, and Amy Flores-Young

Editors: Elizabeth B. Hill, MSW & Mary Ann Pack

Green Heart Living Press

Ignite Your Leadership: Invite Abundance, Increase Income and Impact Our World

Copyright © 2022 Davia H. Shepherd

ISBN (paperback): 978-1-954493-34-6

Cover artwork & Design: Barb Pritchard

GREEN HEART
LIVING
— PRESS —

Dedication

The idea of collaborative leadership or heterarchy means never having to go it alone.

Let's dedicate this book to our amazing supporters who perhaps are the unsung heroes of these stories: Our dear friends and cheerleaders who took our calls and held our hands when we needed it; our families who picked up the slack while we worked in our businesses 24/7; our caring health care providers who helped us through tough times with our mental and physical health; our professional support, who do an outstanding job managing certain details to help our businesses face the public in a seamless way; our collaboration partners, affiliates and ambassadors; our coaches and mentors.

It takes a village to be the right kind of leader, and we dedicate this work to our amazing village!

Selah,
Dr. Davia Shepherd

Table of Contents

Foreword
Wendy Lee   7

Dear Reader
Elizabeth B. Hill, MSW   13

Introduction
Dr. Davia Shepherd   15

Part One: Let it Begin with Me   **19**
Chapter 1: The Secret to Success is Self-Leadership
Pat Alva-Kraker   21

Chapter 2: Unbreakable
Soribel Martinez   29

Chapter 3: She Wouldn't Listen
Brittany Quagan, M.S., LPC   39

Chapter 4: From Grief to Purpose
Leslie M. Gomez   53

Chapter 5: Lead with Joy!
Mary Ann Pack   61

Part Two: Culture Shift   **69**
Chapter 6: An Emerging Culture of Leadership
Cristal L. Cook, LCSW   71

Chapter 7: Leading with IMPACT
Amy Flores-Young   81

Chapter 8: Heart-Led Leadership
Rosemary King   *93*

Part Three: New Organizational Paradigm   **105**
Chapter 9: Cultivating Your Collaborative Team
Shawniel Chamanlal, LCSW   107

Chapter 10: Lead From the Center
Joan Reed Wilson   117

Chapter 11: Growing a Heart-Led Team
Elizabeth B. Hill, MSW   125

Part Four: Leading with Your Own Light   **135**
Chapter 12: Shying Away from the Spotlight
Teresa Hnat   137

Chapter 13: The Power of the Collective
Kathleen Troy   147

Chapter 14: They Called it a Breakdown
Kelly McCarthy   155

Chapter 15: Rebel Yell: Embracing the Leader Within
Barb Pritchard   165

Chapter 16: Heterarchy - An Invitation to Lead in a New Way
Dr. Davia H. Shepherd   175

Foreword

What an honor it is to be a part of *Ignite Your Leadership: Invite Abundance, Increase Income, and Impact the World*. Over the years, I've had countless juicy conversations, some lasting into the wee hours of the night, with my dearest friends, Dr. Davia Shepherd and Elizabeth B. Hill, on this topic. So, when they extended the invitation to write the Foreword, it was an immediate yes. Anytime I get to collaborate with business besties and be in the energy of fabulous women authors, many of whom I know personally, I'm in. I mean, come on, they had me at leadership, a subject that is near and dear to my heart!

I've spent more than two decades in corporate leadership roles and the past five years coaching women, helping them overcome barriers to lead a life and create a living they love. Today I eat, sleep, and breathe leadership. I even incorporated it in the name of my company: LeadHERship Revolution! But I didn't start out with a burning passion for making leadership my life's mission.

I've never considered myself a natural-born leader and preferred to be the worker bee, not the conductor. More of a follower, I led my personal and work life in response to the needs of the people around me. In fact, if you asked the twenty-something version of Wendy if I wanted to pursue a career in leadership, I would have said HELL NO! Ok, maybe that's a little dramatic, but not far from the truth.

I struggled to lead my own damn life, and I had zero confidence in my ability to lead others. Painfully shy, super insecure, and void of any smidgeon of self-worth, I didn't exactly have the makings of a leader. Especially when I compared myself to the managers (they weren't called leaders back then), I saw in positions of power. They seemed so confident and capable.

This was during the mid-eighties. Yes, women were entering the workplace in record numbers, but very few occupied leadership roles. And those that did were operating with the same masculine energy as the predominantly white, older males that called the shots with an authoritarian leadership style. They made decisions without the input of others, and compliance was more out of fear and obligation than inspiration or motivation. It was the norm to take orders, do what you were told, not express an opinion, and follow the rules. A match made in heaven for a people-pleaser like me!

With a start like that, how in the world did I end up as the Senior Vice President of Human Resources and eventually the Founder and CEO of LeadHERship Revolution Coaching and an advocate for shifting the narrative of everything leadership?

I wish I could report that the journey was swift and easy. That overnight, I magically found my inner boss lady and blossomed into a confident, take-charge leader. That wasn't exactly the path I traveled. Admittedly, I took the path of *most* resistance. What I lacked in self-esteem, I made up in pure grit and determination. My insecurity created a longing to be accepted, appreciated, and needed. The only way I knew how to persevere was to be the hardest working at everything I did!

I happily worked overtime and weekends. eagerly took on extra assignments and was always the first to volunteer for special projects. Oh, and by the way, I was simultaneously self-funding my college, fitting in classes at night at the local community college. Of course, nothing but straight A's was good enough for the raging perfectionist in me; anything less resulted in a full-blown meltdown. I was an exemplary student and a model employee. My teachers and bosses loved me. I was a producer, didn't make waves, and went above and beyond. What more could you ask for?

I figured out the formula for leading a successful life was hard work and sacrifice. And the harder I tried, the more praise and recognition I got from society. After eleven years of this routine, I graduated from college and eventually landed in Human Resources.

One rung at a time, I progressed and maneuvered my way up the proverbial corporate ladder. I was promoted from Recruiter to Lead Recruiter to Interim HR Director to HR Director to Vice President of HR and finally arrived at Senior Vice President of Human Resources. I'm exhausted just reading all the effort and time it took to reach that level. After two decades of proving my worth and value, I finally made it to rockstar status.

But I didn't feel like a rockstar. Even with all the success, I still felt a lingering residue of insecurity. I privately second-guessed my ability and didn't always speak up. I micro-managed everything and everyone on my team. I was worn out. Unbeknownst to me, a divine interruption was about to change the trajectory of my life.

My divorce was finalized in the Spring of 2014. Apparently, being a rockstar in business does not guarantee success at home. To put it plainly, I was feeling pretty sh*tty. A reasonable response to a failed marriage, not my first unsuccessful relationship, and a burned-out nervous system, the result of non-stop hustle and grind. I was desperate in search of anything to help make sense of my mess and get some relief.

Plus, I was already in my mid 40s, so my Negative Nancy cheerleader was blasting in my ear that I should have had a better grip on my life by now! Despite the apparent career success and all my efforts, I struggled with feeling sad, lonely, and not good enough. In sheer desperation, I surrendered, threw my hands in the air, and declared out loud: "Something's got to give!"

I started working on myself because I thought I was broken and needed fixing. I read every self-help book, joined the local yoga studio, and started meditating. My quest eventually led me to a transformational retreat in Maui. It wasn't the lounging on the beach and sipping Mai Tais type of retreat. (I wish the path to healing was that easy; that would be avoidance therapy!) It was a transformational retreat facilitated by a life coach.

During the event, I was introduced to the concept of feminine and masculine energy. I realized that I was operating almost entirely in my masculine energy. This was a default survival pattern in response to sexual abuse, abandonment, loss, and neglect trauma that I endured in childhood. Simply having that awareness transformed the way I viewed myself.

For the first time, I felt seen, heard, and validated and had the ability to reclaim my power and choose a different path. Over the course of nearly three decades, I had traded in my authentic self and disconnected from my feelings and emotions. And the shocker was it wasn't because of the corporate environment or my ex-husband; those outside sources were simply mirroring back what was already inside.

I started showing up differently, and my friends, family, and coworkers noticed. Inviting both the masculine and feminine energy to my work and my life created more balance and ease. I let go of the need to strive, and I started to connect more. And you know what happened? People drew closer and wanted to experience what I had. I didn't have to do anything but ignite the spark that was in my heart, and that was enough.

Source has a magical way of stepping in and supporting us when we can't see what's blocking us from greatness. Sometimes it's a whisper, and sometimes it's a smack upside the head. When we get that AHA for ourselves, we show up differently, and the whole paradigm shifts.

What if this is what the last few years have been all about? A way to get us to look at what we can't see in ourselves and grab our attention?

No doubt the pandemic flipped the world upside down. It was especially impactful on women. The unprecedented turn of events magnified and amplified the already present struggles with juggling childcare, career, family, and our health and mental well-being. The concept of life-balance was challenged in ways never seen before. But it also invited us to slow down and reevaluate what matters most.

What if all the unrest, irritation, and uncomfortableness we are experiencing are because we are about to shift into the next evolution of how we identify with and relate to leadership in all areas of our life?

Remember life before the pandemic. Everything was sterile and perfect. We could barely be ourselves at home and didn't dare show or share our personal side at work. Only happy selfies were allowed. Now you can turn up in a virtual meeting with a crying baby in your lap, the dog barking in the background, and your plus one walking by in underwear and not blinking an eye. That's progress, baby!

Leading our lives in fake-ass pretending mode is neither sexy nor sustainable.

What if we start freeing ourselves of this burden and allow others to do the same? Is it possible that starting with ourselves, we could shift the entire leadership narrative?

I'm encouraged by how far we've come and the direction we're going.

Prioritizing mental health. Demanding equal pay and better benefits. Not willing to work decades to move up the ladder or scratch the corporate route altogether and start our own businesses. It all feels like we are taking responsibility for what matters and taking up space.

That is why I am thrilled to see the content of this book. A healthier approach to leadership is emerging, and these insightful, cutting-edge authors are shaking up the norms and shaping the future.

A new approach is on the horizon. Bringing in more feminine energy with collaboration, community, nurturing, compassion, and creativity balances the masculine energy of structure, goals, objective thinking, and stability. A healthier way that ignites the spark in all of us and serves as the beacon to others and the world.

Stop waiting to be healed! Stop waiting to be ready! Grab your imperfections, leverage your past, and show up. It's go-time! We are being called to reimagine leadership, side by side, equally contributing our gifts and talents. Together, we are the change and the creators of leadership reimagined and a better world for all of us.

Wendy Lee
LeadHERship Revolution Coaching

Dear Reader,

You may have grabbed the reigns of leadership, smiling.

You may have had them thrust upon you.

You may be a leader. And not know it.

You may suspect you are, but be shaking in your boots.

We have found a way to lead - and grow - together.

Where we all win at the same time.

You may have been told, like me, that this was impossible.

You may have been told that when one wins, another loses.

Or that when one is in power, another is not.

But these pages hold another way.

We can lead - in partnership - and *all* can win.

We can indeed grow together.

One smile, one word, and one story at a time.

Love & Transformation,
Elizabeth

Introduction

Dr. Davia Shepherd

CHO Ladies' Power Lunch

I was born with this idea. I think you were too. Have you ever felt as though you resonated so deeply with another person, so much so that their successes lit you up as though they were your own, and their struggles felt as deeply rooted as though they were indeed your struggles too?

In our society, it seems ok to feel this way about the ones closest to us - maybe our family. Our parents, spouses, siblings, and children might evoke that kind of feeling in us. But every now and again, we get a glimpse of what is possible. We make a friend who we describe as "like family." Or we have someone who plays a role in our life that might prompt us to say that person was like a mother to me, or we are as close as sisters. If one of those types of connections that we have in life ever needed our support or asked something of us, we would not hesitate. There would be no thought of what's in it for me. No thought of win-win situations, just an innate desire to help in an intentional way and in any way we could. Every so often, we get a glimpse of the connections that exist among all of us.

What if we could feel that level of connection and compassion more often? What if the divisions and separateness that we see out there in our world did not exist at all? What if that simple truth that we all learned in Kindergarten is true? What if we are all one?

I smile as I write this because I remember chatting with one of our amazing Ladies' Power Lunch™ (LPL) members and having her share with me that my ideas about life sound great but that she had been taught that it's "not that simple." I'm here to challenge that a little bit. What if it were that simple? Maybe not easy in its execution, but truly, what if it were that simple?

What if you had the opportunity to be a part of a community where everyone was reaching for that deeper level of connection? What if, through a networking group that you joined to grow your business, you found that, amazingly, you were able to grow in leadership and consciousness as well? What if you found yourself surrounded by people who truly, deeply and intentionally supported you and your business and your growth and development, not from some desire to get something back in return, but because they get it. They understand the deeper connection that exists among us, they understand that this is not a drill, they understand that the time for this type of heartfelt connection is now, and they are ready to play their part in the cosmic dance.

What if you were then able to step into the leadership that has been waiting for you all your life? If you could share your message with a much wider audience, and achieve the impact and reach that your message deserves. Lighting up the folx that truly need you, they, in turn, light up, get their connections to light up too, and exponentially raise the vibration of the planet.

I'm aware that this all sounds very airy-fairy. As a facts and figures girl, a former researcher, this irony is not lost on me. And yet I know this truth as deeply as I am aware of my own beingness: we are all connected, we are all one, and when one is supported, the whole is supported. (Sort of like the Borg but significantly less sinister :)

I am so excited that you are here. I'm excited that you are interested in at least learning more about what it means to lead in a collaborative way. I'm excited that even if you have never considered yourself a leader per se in the old traditional sense, you have picked up this book and that you will have the opportunity to recognize that heterarchy or collaborative leadership speaks directly to your soul. To recognize that we all have a leadership role to play and that in linking arms, we all support each other from our strengths.

Ignite Your Leadership is not just an anthology of inspirational stories and a hands-on experiential summit; it is the embodiment of what happens when women get together. When we do, something magical happens. We tap into a wisdom that we have known for millennia, and we support each other, not because we expect to get something in return, but because we are women, we are here, and we can.

While I have you here, I want to issue a personal invitation for you to join this amazing group of souls that are committed to collaboration and deeper connection: Ladies' Power Lunch™, or LPL, as we call it for short. Our members are the authors of this book you hold in your hand. LPL was born out of six heart-centered women in business, having lunch together in a Ruby Tuesday on Route 6 in Bristol, Connecticut, many years ago. We have grown into a FREE international movement of women with one objective: supporting each other. Bringing together these anthologies is just one of the ways that we share with each other.

If you haven't as yet, I invite you to hop on over and join our free online community. We welcome you!

www.facebook.com/groups/ladiespowerlunch

Part One

Let it Begin with Me

Chapter 1

The Secret to Success is Self-Leadership

Pat Alva-Kraker

Entrepreneurship is in my blood. It began as a young girl growing up in El Paso, Texas. My sister, Corina, and our neighbor, Gussie, and I created a game of "business" that we conducted off of two TV tray tables. One had a register and receipts, the other an industrial supply catalog provided by our dad, who sold industrial supplies. Gussie was the boss with his "office" on his front porch.

The cash register was my favorite toy growing up outside of the Susie Bake Oven. I'd take the orders over the phone, write them up, then walk next door to Gussie's office for approval. Our customer, played by Corina, would come to the "store" to pay and pick up her order.

I fell in love with the art of doing business. My passion was birthed. Looking back over your childhood, when was your passion first revealed to you?

I didn't immediately go into entrepreneurship after college, although the whisper in my ear to follow my passion was always there. I followed a different path before I reconnected with my passion. This happens to a lot of women. We are steered away from childhood passions by society, family, the community, etc. My outside influence came from teachers. After graduating from the University of Texas at El Paso with a BBA, I spent over 35 years working for IBM and Lockheed Martin Aeronautics as a project engineer.

I launched my part-time life coaching business while working in corporate. It transitioned into a full-time business after retirement at the age of 58. Within three years, it expanded to include real estate private lending. I say all this to share one of the many lessons you'll receive in reading my story. Live your passion.

A leader is true to herself.

A leader that is true to herself lives her life according to her values, lives her passion, and does what matters. She doesn't care what others think of her, and she doesn't live her life pleasing others.

As a corporate professional in two male-dominated fields, I found myself sharpening my analytical side of myself because that was what was valued. I am a very intuitive gal, and yet, I put that gift on the back burner.

Over time, I realized that I wasn't bringing all of myself to the table. I began to invest in myself. I hired a coach, took personal development classes, and began to teach what I needed most to learn. I began to lead myself better. I learned to integrate my analytical and intuitive sides of me to make decisions. Now, I make heart-centered decisions, and I check in with my intuition all the time. Although I still use data as part of my decision-making process, it no longer guides my decisions. I trust my inner guidance above all else. Now, I move forward with confidence.

A leader brings all of who she is to the table and relies on her inner guidance to make decisions.

Do you feel like you're bringing in all of who you are to the table? You know, the analytical part of who you are that most of corporate America foster *and* the intuitive self that it doesn't. Eventually, you know within that something is missing. There's more to you that's not showing up. I mentor women on self-trust and self-leadership. As I work with women leaders, we begin to uncover where they show up fully and where they don't. I teach them how to follow their inner knowing and honor their specific decision-making process. When you know your specific decision-making process, you don't miss opportunities, you sleep at night knowing your decisions align with your values, and you don't second guess yourself.

A leader practices self-care daily.

My life changed when in 1996 when I learned I had breast cancer. I was stopped in my tracks! Filled with uncertainty and fear, I felt the universe was asking me to take a pause, evaluate the way I was living my life, and adjust. I was burning the candles on both ends, giving to everyone except myself. I wasn't practicing self-care. I see this trend in my clients. Running a business is demanding. You must be at your best every day, and that requires self-care. It's a necessity.

Self-care is a set of activities you practice daily that supports the lifestyle you've always dreamed of and includes activities that keep you healthy, feed your soul and expand your mind. I have provided some suggestions further down in this chapter, where we jointly create a morning routine.

I believe in "constant and never-ending improvement," a term coined by Tony Robbins. I consistently invest in myself. I learned that success in my business is directly connected to my personal growth.

A leader consistently invests in herself.

Attending conferences, reading books, listening to podcasts, and hiring a coach are a few ways to invest in yourself.

When I stepped into my business full-time, I realized I had to change my morning routine to support my new role. So, I began to create a holistic routine. A routine that included exercise, learning something new every day, keeping myself focused on my goals, feeding my soul, and allowing me to learn from each day's experiences.

A leader begins her day with an empowering morning routine.

Here's what my morning routine looks like today.

1. Meditation
2. Saying affirmations out loud
3. Reading my goals and visualizing my day
4. Identifying the three things I need to do today to reach my goals
5. Exercising
6. Learn something new (listen to a podcast, read or watch a YouTube video
7. Journaling

The benefits of a morning routine include:
- Feeling centered and empowered
- Waking up energized and focused
- Being in a state of gratitude and forward movement

Create a morning routine that resonates with you. Keep it simple, try different activities and be consistent. Use some of the elements from my routine to get started. You can create a routine that takes 15 minutes.

A leader lives her life according to her Human Design for Business.

All of us are born with a specific blueprint that guides us in life and in business. A blueprint that tells us how we are meant to make decisions show up in the world and be successful in business, for starters. When you discover what makes you unique, you give yourself permission to be you, and with that comes a life of ease, grace, and greater fulfillment. My clients thrive once they better understand themselves. I use a tool and system called Human Design for Business to help women understand themselves and embrace their essence. It is a synthesis of ancient and modern sciences and is a valuable tool for personal and team development. If you're interested in learning about your unique Human Design blueprint, go to www.hdforbusinessbook.com and schedule a Human Design for Business Overview with me.

Self-Leadership Principles

The self-leadership principles I have shared with you have contributed to my success as a leader, entrepreneur, wife, sister, and friend. If you took one of the principles of the chapter and practiced it for 30 days with consistency and discipline, you will feel more confident and aligned and experience a greater sense of peace, satisfaction, and success.

The passion for "business" first discovered as a child has evolved into working with women entrepreneurs to develop their self-leadership skills. Most are women who have plateaued in their business and want to express their passion and elevate their business. After working with me, my clients experience an increase in profits, greater productivity, and an increase in team performance.

"When you discover what makes you unique, you give yourself permission to be you, and with that comes a life of ease, grace, and greater fulfillment."

~Pat Alva-Kraker

About Pat Alva-Kraker

Pat Alva-Kraker is an award-winning business consultant, mentor, real estate private lender, and philanthropist. She has combined 35 years in corporate America as an IT project engineer, ranching, and real estate industries. She assists heart-centered women entrepreneurs to scale their businesses with ease and grace, so they can experience time and financial freedom and create a life they love.

Pat is a business catalyst speaker and trainer. She speaks on mindful leadership, self-care done easy, and the power of knowing your decision-making strategy.

Pat is the author of the #1 best-seller *Katherine's Quest: One Woman's Journey to Elation* and three best-selling collaboration books. Pat has been recognized by Women of Color, Leadership Texas, and the Hispanic Women's Network of Texas for her passion for developing women leaders. She lives in Fort Worth with her husband, Mitch, and their dog, Dakota.

Connect with Pat:

www.MajesticCoachingGroup.com

www.twitter.com/PatAlvaKraker

www.linkedin.com/in/patalvakraker/

www.facebook.com/majesticcoaching/

www.linkedin.com/company/majestic-coaching-group-llc/

www.instagram.com/patalvakraker

www.pinterest.com/patalvakraker

Notes

Chapter 2

Unbreakable

Soribel Martinez

I switched off my car's engine and zipped my coat in anticipation of the autumn chill. Leaves danced from the trees landing on the hood of my Lincoln Navigator, and I couldn't help but feel thankful I was about to leave behind the chilly wind for a few days of warmth and relaxation in Panama. My son John Anthony and I just needed a few more things to be ready for our flight, and I was anxious to get in and out of the mall quickly before picking him up from the Montessori school he attended. Shopping with a two-and-a-half-year-old in tow isn't something any mother can master.

My phone chimed in my pocketbook, and I pulled it out to see my doctor's office name flash across the screen.

"Hello."

"Hi, is Ms. Martinez available?" a deep male voice asked.

"May I ask who's calling?"

"It's Doctor Sythe."

"This is she," I glanced at my watch, conscious of the time.

"Hi. This is Doctor Sythe. I'm calling with the results of your MRI. Unfortunately, your MRI shows that you don't have just one but two aneurysms. We need to sit down and discuss the next steps."

My heart sped up. A roaring in my ears drowned out the doctor's voice. I was in shock. I was confused and frozen.

He talked about life-threatening risks, surgery, and recovery

29

time, but none of it entered my consciousness. My mind could focus only on the life-threatening dangers of surgery and making it through recovery time while caring for a young boy. My Aunt Celia had gone through similar surgery years prior - I knew how serious this was.

I sat frozen in the driver's seat. I looked down at my phone still in my hand and knew I needed to reach out for support. I called my mom, then my dad, and my Aunt Celia, who'd had a brain aneurysm burst during her last trimester with her youngest child and needed surgery, to let them know the news. I didn't know what I would do next, but I knew I'd need my people around me to get through it. I was supposed to be going to Panama with my little boy and our friends. I was supposed to be living life, not fighting for it.

I'd have to put my life on hold in the coming months. I'd need to take time away from work, call on my family to hold me up, and explain to a child whose mama was his whole world why we needed to stop breastfeeding abruptly. But at that moment, it was just me and my grief sitting in my SUV, wind whipping leaves through the air, and the sun setting in the distance. Time stopped.

The trip to Panama was forgotten - I left the shopping mall parking lot and drove to pick up John Anthony on autopilot. All I could think about was death and how unfair it was that I would have to leave my son motherless. It was terrible. I couldn't focus on work, and I went through the motions at home, dressing my boy and making his favorite foods - even playing with him - but my mind wasn't really present. Grief for a life I thought I'd never have consumed me.

I received a letter from my doctor's office a few days later.

Ms. Martinez, it is imperative that you give us a call and schedule a follow-up appointment with Dr. Sythe to discuss your treatment options. This is a very serious health matter, and you must give us a call.

I couldn't shake the fog of grief. I couldn't bring myself to act. A psychologist said, "Soribel, if you think you are going to die, you are going to die. You need to transform your mindset, perception, and how you see this crisis in your life."

Her words were 100% correct. Nothing we experience in life - no matter how difficult - can steal our fire unless we let it. Adversity does not destroy you - it teaches you a lesson, transforms you, and redirects you toward your true purpose. I decided I needed to find a way to fight; I needed to trust something greater than myself and have the strength to ask for help. That's the only way to get through life - trust your path, fight like hell, and don't ever try to go it alone.

I embarked on a mission to find the best possible solution to the aneurysms. I refused to accept anything except survival. I traveled to specialists in New York, Ohio, and Florida searching for someone who would confidently operate and save my life. I finally settled on having surgery with Dr. Krarushig in Harford, CT.

In July 2010, I scheduled an appointment with my stylist. I knew my hair needed to be shaved for surgery, and I decided to regain some of the power I felt I'd lost. I wanted a sliver of control in a situation that felt completely out of hand. My stylist cut and styled my hair short so I didn't have to deal with the emotional toll of losing that piece of myself in the sterile walls of a hospital. The doctor operated on my brain on September 24, 2010. And, like a miracle, I went home three days later, walked on my own, talked, and was able to hug my little boy. I was ready to continue the fight.

I reflect on those moments every day. The brain aneurysms served as a sort of wake-up call. I was going through life, but I wasn't seizing my purpose and making the impact I wanted in this world. I'd see women struggling like me - single mothers working full-time jobs and trying to be everything to their tiny people. I was sick of struggling all the time. I wished I could do more to help other people and help correct the society that makes women feel like they can never be or do enough. I wasn't following my path because I'd stopped listening to the source of my power, creator, and God, and started listening to everyone around me.

I'm not saying that having brain surgery was a positive experience. It was hell on earth battling for my life. I still remember when three-year-old John Anthony looked at my stitches and said, "Mami, you look like a monster." My heart broke, and though I was sad but healing, finding a path to health and living long enough to raise my son demanded that I reconnect to that higher power, and in doing so, I found my true path to service, success, and happiness. I needed to connect to my creator to grow into leadership.

To reconnect with my God, I needed to unlearn all the lessons I learned from organized religion growing up. I had to heal from religious trauma and understand that God doesn't have anything to do with other people who hurt me. It didn't matter if I went to church every Sunday, sang a single hymn, or prayed over each meal - what mattered was that I connected with God in meaningful ways.

I feel most connected to God when I'm helping people create the lives they want and teaching others. When I'm working in alignment with my purpose, I feel energized, and I also get compensated well. Success is evidence of that alignment.

When I need to talk to God, I journal and ask him to show me the right path and the people who will help me along the way. He's never misguided me. When I'm in quiet solitude, and my mind can focus inward, I can find the next right step. Focusing on God helps me take that step in confidence without worrying about the big-picture-fear that tries to creep in and derail my efforts. Most of my next steps come to me in the shower - I'm sure there's some connection between the cleansing energy and my ability to hear Him.

Those moments when I know my next right step aren't free of fear - that's a common misconception about leaders. We are afraid every day. We're scared of failing, of letting down those who depend on us for employment and sustenance, of abandoning ourselves in the process. Being a leader means that when your decisions align with your purpose and core values, you feel empowered, and that empowerment is bigger than any fear.

After recovering from surgery, I became an overworked single mother struggling to make ends meet. I worked as a school social worker and felt as if I was drowning as I tried to keep up with the costs of raising a young man. I asked God to show me the path out of my financial struggles. And finally, after months of desperate prayer, journaling, and meditation, I had an overwhelming feeling that I needed to start a private therapy practice.

In summer 2018, I prepared for the clinical social work exam and passed it at the end of August, just as a new school year started. I started that year but knew I wouldn't stay through June. I began seeing clients in the evenings and on weekends and had a waitlist so long that I knew I needed to leave the school system and dive headfirst into scaling my practice. So, with the school principal telling me I wouldn't make it and the school district begging me to reconsider, I left, and I've never looked back.

As a leader, each decision I make must align with my values. The first of those is the importance of family. As the first person in my family to finish high school, graduate from college, and complete advanced degree programs, I always felt an obligation to continue building the life my ancestors opened the doors to. I made this decision when I was seven years old. I knew I needed to be an influential leader, impact the world, and open doors for the family coming after me.

My grandfather moved from the Dominican Republic to New York as an undocumented immigrant and worked to achieve legal status before bringing my grandmother and their children, one of whom was my father. It wasn't until 1988 that my father could get my mother to the United States, leaving my two brothers and me in the Dominican Republic with an aunt for a year. When I opened my practice, I wanted to create a business that aligned with my purpose and allowed me to give my son all the opportunities he could wish for. I want other women, especially women of color, to see me and know they can achieve greatness.

Another value that guides my decision-making as a leader and business owner is collaboration. Even early on, I knew I couldn't run a business without a team. To align with my purpose, I need to focus on my genius work - being a therapist. So, I hired people to do all the other pieces of the business to keep my focus. My team included a billing department to handle insurance claims, an accountant to keep track of the financials, and a lawyer.

In addition to a team to handle the business details, I worked with a business coach from the beginning. I believe investing in yourself is a sign of self-love and is the best way to stay focused on your purpose, identify your next steps, and stay accountable to your action plan. I've continued to invest in business coaching through every step of scaling my practice. None of us can create the life of our dreams without calling on others for support.

Leaders are givers. We seek to support others, smooth the path for people coming behind us, and give back to our communities. We cannot do that well if we aren't whole, happy, healthy people. In entrepreneurship, there's this idea that you have to work on your business at all costs. People sacrifice their physical, emotional, and mental health in the name of success and wealth.

I've experienced first-hand the terrifying reality of what happens if we don't care for ourselves. If I'd ignored my doctor's phone call, if I hadn't listened to the voice of my creator telling me I hadn't yet fulfilled my purpose, I wouldn't have found the strength to fight.

As a leader, I don't hesitate to take the necessary time to take care of myself. Sure, I work hard and live my life full of passion and energy, but no amount of passion can keep us from being human. We need rest, we get sick, and we need to move our bodies and nourish them as best we can. Being a leader requires that you fuel yourself so you can inspire others. As soon as I started taking care of myself first and made loving myself my top priority, my business blossomed.

When you work from a place of purpose and service to others, you find alignment. This alignment creates a cyclical dance from purpose to creation to success. Money is a result of the energy of that alignment. When you're focused on making a positive impact in your community, working with passion and energy, and taking care of yourself, you'll reach levels of success you never thought possible.

I invite you to step into leadership by getting quiet enough to find your purpose and aligning your life and decisions to that genius. Whether you want to run a therapy practice, run a non-profit, or create a coaching business, working in alignment with your purpose will ensure you achieve the level of success you crave. Maximize your impact in the community, maximize your freedom, and maximize your success by aligning your work to your true purpose.

None of us works well in a vacuum. People need people - and that's true no matter how fiercely independent you are. When you're building a business, you'll need to find people who support you (and spend less time with those who don't). You'll need a team of people to help you build the business of your dreams so you can focus on your genius work, and you'll need mentors and coaches to help you stay accountable to your action plan.

When I work with my private practice coaching clients, I start by asking them the following questions. I've included them here so you can start thinking about your purpose and how your business aligns with that goal.

- **When do you feel the most energized?** Passion and energy is God's way of directing you toward your true path. Pay attention to when you find yourself "in the zone" - that space where you can work for hours, forget to eat, and not feel overwhelmed.

- **What contribution or impact would you like to make in this world?** Maybe you have a vision related to health and wellness, or maybe you dream of helping pull people out of poverty. Your desired impact should drive your business decisions.

- **What people in your life are positive influences and supports in your entrepreneurial journey?** Do you need to find more people? What types of people do you need around you?

To take a deeper dive into finding your purpose and take the next steps in your entrepreneurial journey, I invite you to download my free workbook listed below.

www.bit.ly/LiveYourPurposeWorkbook

"Leaders are givers. We seek to support others, smooth the path for people coming behind us, and give back to our communities. We cannot do that well if we aren't whole, happy, healthy people."

~Soribel Martinez

About Soribel Martinez

Soribel is a psychotherapist with over 20 years of experience in the mental health field who recently sought certification as a sex coach through the Institute for Sexuality. She's conducted therapy in schools, homes, and outpatient programs and is experienced working with people of all ages.

Soribel holds a master's degree in psychology and social work from the University of Southern California. She is the CEO of SMPsychotherapy & Counseling Services, and as a business owner, she understands the demands of building a business while trying to create fulfilling relationships.

Soribel's work as a concierge therapist allows her to take fewer clients than traditional therapists so she can offer individualized attention as well as the latest techniques in psychotherapy and mental health care.

A life-long learner and lover of education, Soribel offers sex education and female empowerment programs to schools, businesses, and mental health professionals. She also works as an associate psychology professor at Post University.

Connect with Soribel:

www.SoribelMartinez.com

Live Your Purpose Workbook:
www.bit.ly/LiveYourPurposeWorkbook

Notes

Chapter 3

She Wouldn't Listen

Brittany Quagan, M.S., LPC

I **am nine years old.** I'm sitting on my bedroom floor, back against my bed, tongue hanging out the side of my mouth as I exercise all of my focus on drawing out my business logo. I have just spent the last few hours dreaming up the *perfect* business plan, down to the client intake forms. I will open up a salon and spa above the red barn that houses the tractor, tools, and a dozen bats on our property. My dad will build it for me because he knows how to do those things, so it should be easy.

People from all over the state will come here to relax, to feel beautiful and powerful. *It will be amazing.* I smile to myself. I finish filling in the lens on the sunglasses hanging over the sun's smiling face. *Sunblast Salon.* I grab my packet of materials and run down the hall to show my family. I am met with an unenthusiastic "yeah, ok" from my parents. "You're only nine, you idiot; it'll never work," my brother adds.

I am ten years old. The holidays are around the corner, and I have noticed we have the ideal yard for a show-stopping light display. I frantically get out my art supplies and begin sketching out my idea for a giant cutout of five people, representing our family, that waves their arms and brings cheer to all who drive by. I just need to figure out how to make them bigger, keep them from getting wet in the rain since I only have cardboard, and establish how we will light them up. I bring my genius idea to my dad.

"What?!" he asks, almost exasperated. "We can't do that."

I am 13 years old. My best friend and I are dying to go to an overnight camp in North Carolina where they film *Bug Juice*, a reality television show on the Disney channel that focuses on a tween drama-filled campground.

"You guys don't understand. This is my chance to be famous!" I plead. This is all that is standing in my way of fulfilling my dream of becoming an actress.

"Brittany," they say, annoyed. "It's never going to happen. You're not going to get famous. You wouldn't make it one night at that camp, either. You're a baby who's too scared to leave home. You're not going."

"Yeah, idiot," my little brother chimes in.

I am 18 years old when my dad asks me what my plan is for my life.

"I'm going to become a famous author," I say confidently as if there is no other possible scenario for my future.

"Come on," he scoffs. "You live in a la-la land."

It's true. I think to myself. *I can't even go to college; how could I be a famous author?* My panic attacks keep me from going anywhere alone or far from home. I haven't even driven a car without anyone else in it in months.

I am 26 years old. The birds outside are singing loudly and stir me from my sleep. As I realize that it is morning, I rise with a start and quickly look to my left to ensure my boyfriend is sleeping still.

I sigh internally for a brief moment. *Thank goddess. There is still time.*

I attempt with all of my willpower to make myself as weightless as possible as I creep from the bed and out the door of the bedroom, careful to tiptoe on the creaky floors and stairs. I get to the shower and move through it as quickly as I can.

STOMP.

Fuck. My breath picks up. *No. no. no.*

I have learned to read his movements, his posture, his schedule – all to prepare me for what my day will be like. I hear him descend down the stairs, and my heart plummets to my stomach as he starts to hammer down on the door, rattling at the locked doorknob intermittently. I back up slowly.

"OPEN THIS FUCKING DOOR!" he screams from the other side. I open it slowly to eyes boring down at me as if I am nothing. "LOOK AT THIS FUCKING MESS. LOOK AT IT!" he points to the kitchen around the corner.

I try to calm him down and explain that the bottle of oven cleaner I used the night before said to leave it on overnight before wiping it out, but his temper is already through the roof. I notice the sponge on the sink, an arm's length away, and I grab it and move toward the oven to show him I am willing to do it.

"Please just let me do this!"

He moves out of the way, and I drop to my knees and start scrubbing. He starts to walk, and my muscles tense in response, unsure, until I hear that they are moving in the opposite direction, hopeful that that was the end of it. Not even a minute later, he returns, anger amplified.

"I'M SICK AND TIRED OF ALWAYS BEING THE ONE TO CLEAN THIS FUCKING PLACE UP. DO YOU KNOW HOW MUCH WORK I HAVE TO DO TODAY? I DON'T HAVE TIME FOR THIS SHIT! YOU'RE FUCKING USELESS!" he bends down to scream in my face. "AND I GUESS I'LL DO THE LAUNDRY...AGAIN! DO YOU EVEN PAY FOR THE LAUNDRY DETERGENT IN THIS HOUSE? FUCKING PRINCESS. SITS ON HER FUCKING THRONE AND GETS WHATEVER THE FUCK SHE WANTS. NO WONDER YOUR EX CHEATED ON YOU; YOU FUCKING SUCK!!"

One arm wipes at my running nose while the other feels like it might break from the pressure I am putting on it to scrub, scrub, scrub.

"AND YOU THINK I'LL MARRY SOMEONE LIKE YOU?" he laughs. "YOU'RE FUCKING INSANE! I WOULD NEVER MARRY YOU. EVER!"

He marches passed me, looks at me, and mutters, "pathetic," before ripping the front door open, slamming it behind him, and leaving.

When I hear his car start and pull away, I drop to my hip and weep.

I am 26 years old. I have been working at an insurance company for the last four years and hating every second of it, except for happy hours. I've spent the last two years exploring spirituality as part of my quest to heal from debilitating anxiety and panic attacks. I have since gotten Reiki certified and begun giving readings at psychic home parties on the weekends. I find that I am really good at what I do. Aside from the deep knowing of what someone has gone through in their life, I have the ability to make them feel better and more empowered.

I decide this is what I want to do with my life. To heal people. The company I work for announces we are getting laid off in six months, and rather than look for a job in insurance (or elsewhere), I start to build up my business. I create a website; my dad builds a healing room for me to work out of in the back of my mom's salon; I blog weekly and create a book of business.

It is now two months after opening the doors to my first healing center, and I am actually succeeding. I'm standing in my retail room, surrounded by beautiful crystals, books, tarot cards, and tinctures, and I am chatting on the phone with my dad about LLCs versus S-Corps. After a few moments of silence, he asks, "When are you going to get a real job?"

My open house is the next day. There are so many people we have to turn sideways to walk passed one another. My space is full of people, love, laughter, and tears of joy. Everyone who enters paints their hand and presses it against the canvas with a pre-painted tree on it, their hands representing the leaves. I hang this at the front of the center at the end of the night.

I take a look around at the sea of people surrounding me, smiling from ear to ear. I notice one person missing from the crowd. My dad. I feel my smile waver but shake my head, take a deep breath in and walk over to some new faces to introduce myself.

I'm 29 years old. I am nearly done with my master's degree in clinical counseling. All that is left is to secure an internship to get some clinical hours under my belt. On a whim, I contact a doctor at Yale School of Medicine whom I had connected to when I participated in a research study he led. The worst that can happen is he tells me to kick rocks. My heart races and feels as though it has lodged itself into my throat when I read his reply email.

"Of course, I remember you! I would love to meet and discuss this further. When might you be available to come to campus and get coffee?"

Oh, my goddess. He wants to meet. He took my email seriously.

Panic courses through my veins throughout the entire drive, and walk to the donut shop where I am meeting this doctor. He greets me with an enthusiastic smile and hug as I enter the shop, and we head to the counter to order drinks and donuts before sitting down.

He appears very interested in what I have to say about mental health, the spiritual flair I bring to my healing sessions, and how I feel mental health care needs to change - topics I am deeply passionate about outwardly. I can feel the conversation is coming to a close and my heart rate picks up again, knowing we are about to talk about the reason I came here - a random intuitive healer turning therapist seeking an internship *at an Ivy League freakin school*. He shares his interests with me as well and the research steps he wants to take.

The study I participated in a few years prior was focusing on individuals who have auditory hallucinations, or as I like to call them, perceptual experiences, but don't have a diagnosis or need any clinical care. As an intuitive person who offers readings to my clients, of course, I hear things - and feel them - and see them. The energy I refer to as my guides tell me things all the time. He was fascinated by the fact that people could have these experiences and fully control them or not be distressed by them. My guides only talk when I'm in danger or when I ask them to. I never needed to care for them and never have had any scary or distressing experiences with them, either.

"How would you feel about teaming up together to help me lead a study on these experiences?" he asks.

This is my chance. This is my time to bring change to the mental health system. To infiltrate psychiatry from the inside out and help people with unusual experiences feel normal.

Six months pass, and I've been actively interning for the doctor. I am not only learning every aspect of research I could possibly learn, but I'm learning how to assess young people who are at risk of developing more serious mental illnesses and learning how to work with them therapeutically, enhancing my clinical skills.

I'm out to dinner with my dad and talking about my exciting internship at Yale. I can't wait to tell him how the doctor told me he'd love to hire me for a full-time job. My body is buzzing with excitement over this achievement.

My dad takes a sip of his bloody mary. "Well, you should have gone to school at Yale. That would be something."

The high vibrations filling me ceased immediately as if I were unplugged from a wall socket. It took me a moment to gather my thoughts and not immediately explode into anger-filled tears.

"Isn't the point of going to a fancy Ivy League school to get a good job? Well, I'm getting the good job."

"Ehhhh..." he shakes his head. "No, because what if you wanted to switch jobs to Harvard or another big school? You probably can't because you don't have a school like that on your resume."

My voice is caught in my throat, and I no longer felt emboldened. "I feel like there is nothing I can do or say to make you just be proud of me," I quietly say.

"It's not that," he says dismissively. "I'm just saying."

The waiter comes over to hand us our bill, signaling that it's time for us to go.

I am 30 years old. I have been told throughout my entire life all that I am incapable of and all that I will never be able to accomplish. I have been reminded through repeated, related experiences that I am never going to be good enough – all of which have set the tone for my inner narrative.

I have spent my entire existence on this earth taking lefts, pivoting right, and darting in every possible direction to try and keep up with all of the things that others want me to. To prove that I am worth it. To prove that I am somebody.

"I'm bad,"

"I'm wrong."

"I'm foolish."

"I'm crazy."

"I'm nothing."

My dad told me when I was 20 years old to work in a corporate environment, climb the ladder, and focus on job security when I wanted to move to Vermont or California for writing school. He also encouraged me to change my major to business when I wanted to focus on psychology. Pivot. Pivot.

45

Anxiety. Anxiety. Wrong direction. Wrong direction.

My mom told me to find a nice Italian man who would marry me when I was 22, so I could hurry up and have kids because "my eggs were getting scrambled," and so I found and stayed with one because this was the path I'm "supposed" to take.

Any opportunity that sounded *successful* and financially secure I fled for because my mind told me, after a lifetime of conditioning, that that is what I *had* to do - or *else*.

I am sitting in my office, tongue hanging out of my mouth, as I write up notes on a talk I will be giving on healing from anxiety and trauma at a Happiness conference. As I write, I am struck with ideas for a new workshop to teach and am filled with excitement to offer this to the world. I look up and around the room for a brief moment as if searching for someone to tell about my idea. I settle back into my seat with a smile, realizing that I don't need anyone to validate my idea as good enough, and continue to write.

It is hour three of the spiritual expo we are working on. There is a line of at least fifteen people waiting to spin the jeopardy wheel we have brought for our booth and win a prize. A woman approaches me and asks what it is that we do at Journeys: School for the Soul.

"We offer readings, healings, and coaching," I share with her. "We help you embrace your superpower."

Her smile widens as she puts her name on the sign-up sheet for a reading. "Will you be doing readings today?" she asks me. I've now received this question for the hundredth time.

"Not today." I look over to my right, where four out of seven of the women of Journeys are giving healing and empowering messages to clients. This weekend is about them, for them to grow their business and showcase their talents. I can't help but beam with excitement and gratitude, not only at what I have built but to have been able to watch these women grow so exponentially from students to business owners. Life often feels surreal – that the girl whose ideas were too big, too dumb, the girl who thought she was nothing, could turn that pain into her power and help others rise up from theirs to do the same. "One of these amazing women is sure to change your life."

I am in my 30s. I am standing in the bathroom of a hotel in downtown New Haven looking at myself in the mirror. I take a sip of my celebratory tequila seltzer and smile. My heart is still racing from the adrenaline of sitting on a panel at yet another conference – this time surrounded not only by clients there to listen but mental health professionals, including world-renowned psychiatrists and psychologists in the field. I think back to the hundreds of eyes that were on me just an hour or two beforehand – hands in the air, eager to ask me my thoughts, my opinions, my ideas. I shake my head in disbelief while wiping at the tear in the corner of my eye.

I am reminded that just because I still hear the negative comments and opinions – does not mean that I have to listen. Every comment is a reminder that I will never be who they want me to be – a reminder of the choice I had to make. I could either never be who they want me to be – and continue to try, to pivot, continue to be full of pain as I do; or I could never be who they want me to be – and follow my drumbeat, my path, my dreams. The road that brought me here. To this moment.

"I am bad, wrong, foolish, crazy, nothing" has shifted with every step I take into alignment – as I feel better, stronger, and more empowered, I see better, I see good, I see right, I see knowledgeable, I see passionate, I see grounded, I see everything, I see me.

I am talking with one of my closest friends, who is also a healer. Our jokes about relating to *Alice in Wonderland* and Dorothy

Gale for all the "crazy" stuff they've seen turn into a brainstorming session to ideas pitching for ways to help normalize spiritual thought in a field that likes to label people. We are not the only ones who work as advocates in this way, but we have a community of empowering humans who are doing this work – a validating community that I find vital to my well-being.

I have spent my life being told who I am and who I am not. I've been told what I am capable of, of what is possible, and I have followed the instruction of those who have inserted their opinions and ideas on what my life should and shouldn't be. Through these experiences, I have learned that fear can force us to feel we have to turn outward to get our answers — that our internal dialogue can not be trusted, and therefore, we are not to be trusted to make the decisions that shape our lives.

My father's opinions dictated my life for years. "Get your foot in the door at a good company and climb the ladder," he'd say. "A steady, stable paycheck." I reluctantly obliged, certain that my smart, financially savvy father must know more than my 20-year-old self and be setting me up for success. When they laid off our entire company, I also realized that there is no such thing as steady, and just because he is my father, that does not make him always right, no matter what I wanted to believe.

Another day full of sessions and of learning has arrived. Although I am "supposed to be" the "expert," I am continuously gaining just as much from my clients as they gain from our work together – from their stories, their experiences, and most, from the regular reminder that I am not, in fact, an expert on someone else's life. My role is not to tell someone what to do, what decisions to make, or who they are to become. I am here to help my clients learn that they are the CEOs of their own life – that they do, in fact, know what is best for themselves and how to move through the anxious thoughts that tell them otherwise.

It can be a terrifying thing – recognizing our own power. To learn that we have the ability to dictate our own lives means that we don't actually have to suffer as long as we have been, and that is why I am present in my clients' lives. To aid them in the exploration of options, to support them as the fear sets in, and to remind them of what they are capable of. That is, after all, what leaders do – leaders are those who have recognized that they do not have to follow and who help others recognize the same.

It is today.

Sunblast Salon has a different name and location but a similar mission.

The books have been and continue to be written.

I am not famous, but folx have come to hear me speak and tell my story.

I am worthy of being married and am happily married to an incredible human being. My life is my own, and I give myself permission to keep it that way.

"It can be a terrifying thing – recognizing our own power. To learn that we have the ability to dictate our own lives means that we don't actually have to suffer as long as we have been."

~Brittany Quagan, M.S., LPC

About Brittany Quagan, M.S., LPC

Brittany Quagan is a Yale School of Medicine trained licensed therapist, intuitive healer, and life coach. Through her experiences with mental health and trauma, she found healing in spiritual practices, meditation, mindfulness, and guides who helped her to challenge her limiting beliefs. Helping others to find peace and empowerment as she did became her life's work.

What once started as a spiritual & healing center, Journeys: School for the Soul in Windsor, CT, and Journeys: Holistic Wellness & Anxiety Relief Center in Simsbury, CT, have since evolved to an online experience where Brittany offers both spiritual healing, life coaching, classes, mentorship, and counseling. She specializes in EMDR, CBT, DBT, and narrative therapies for anxiety, trauma, depression, relationships, and women's empowerment.

Connect with Brittany:

www.BrittanyQuaganCounseling.com

Notes

Chapter 4

From Grief to Purpose

Leslie Gomez

One of the experiences in my life that has shaped my current career the most was having a child with special needs. At the age of 27 years old, I discovered that I was pregnant with my second child. This pregnancy was unplanned as I recently started my new career as a registered nurse. I had a slew of plans for my life as I approached this new chapter, but God had other plans for me.

I went through most of my pregnancy with ease. All blood, prenatal and genetic testing were normal. I was eagerly planning for the arrival of my healthy, typical baby. At 28 weeks gestation, I started to have complications that were in no relation to the final diagnosis of my baby. I was diagnosed with placenta previa. I was placed on bed rest for the duration of my pregnancy. My doctor told me if I rebleed, I would need an emergency c-section. Well, it happened again a month before his due date; they decided it was safe for him to be delivered. I was super excited to meet my bundle of joy. I couldn't wait to hold and kiss him. At 36 weeks gestation, I safely delivered my baby via c-section.

I waited impatiently to hold him. He was finally placed in my arms as I prepped to start breastfeeding. My husband and I cuddled him, kissed him, and examined him from head to toe, all while fighting over his resemblance. He had all ten fingers and all ten toes. When I arrived on the postpartum floor after delivery, I met up with a nurse friend that I had worked with for years; let's call her Jan. Jan took care of me while at the hospital. I can clearly remember her taking my baby back to the nursery to be examined and weighed. She never came back into the room, I would ring the bell for assistance, and she would not come as she did previously. The CNA was sent in each time. I wondered where she had gone as I did not see her again.

The doctor came in to check on mom and baby. With baby in hand, he says, "Mr. and Mrs. Gomez, your baby has Down syndrome." I was dumbfounded. Everything he said after that was like the teacher from Charlie Brown, and it was at that very moment that I felt my heart fall to the bottom of my stomach, and it stayed there. I was in total shock to the point that I couldn't even cry. After the doctor left the room, denial set in. My husband and I examined him again from head to toe, but all we saw was a six pounds of cuteness overload. I hugged him. The tears started to flow.

Hours after the gut-wrenching news that robbed me of happiness, all I could think of was how I was going to protect this innocent soul from the world. How was I going to take care of someone so fragile? How was I going to explain this to my precious 6-year-old daughter, who also waited for the arrival of her little brother? It was a lot that we as a family had to learn. My husband comforted me and ensured that Jeyden was going to be just fine. I can remember him saying, "Leslie, he could have cancer or something much worse. He has all his fingers and all his toes. We are in this together...ten toes down, let's go. A couple of days later, we were discharged home.

I wasn't prepared. I was still in shock. I didn't know where to start. My heart just told me to love him and treat him like I would any other child. That was the blueprint we used up until this day. We focused on his strengths, and we worked on his weaknesses, promising to help him live his life to his full potential.

It was a tough six months ahead for me. Work was my escape, but when I came home, I cried. I cried every day. I was angry. I felt like God had punished me, not knowing he really sent an angel. I couldn't see anything different at this time. I had to stay strong for my family. I had a very compassionate and understanding husband that helped me through. When I had a negative thought, he would alter it with a positive perspective.

It took a very long time for me to deal with my feelings. I would bring Jeyden places, and Mama Bear would be activated. It was clear to family and friends not to treat him differently. Don't ask any questions. Conversations about him were difficult and minimal (in the aspect of diagnosis). In my eyes, he was just like anyone else. His diagnosis did not matter. When Jeyden was 12 years old, I could finally have a conversation about him without tearing up and crying.

Throughout the years, I went through the five stages of grief; denial, anger, bargaining, depression, and acceptance. I grieved the loss of a typical child. It was tough. Tough on my family. Many years went by, and it was like I was in a fog and just going through the daily motions. My baby girl lost her mom for a little bit, but she had no problem jumping right into the routine.

With my grief came a deeper love for people. Regardless of who they were and what they were going through. I learned to love people for who they were and for where they were in their life. No judgment, just meeting them where they were at. I realized that everyone was imperfect and divinely made.

Jeyden ultimately gave me the strength to love people and look at people in a different light. I learned to meet people where they were and find the wanting to help see what they couldn't see for themselves, to deliver the vision, the vision that they had for themselves. I wanted to help them understand that although things happen to them in their lives, that doesn't mean it ends there.

My purpose was clearly defined. My purpose was to help, empower, and heal. First with my hands, now through my lens. So through this particular journey, I just connected what I was put on this earth to do.

Before I could help, I had to heal myself, and photography helped me do just that. Photography is where I found my peace, my tranquility, and my power.

My journey and my camera allowed me to understand who and what I wanted to be known for. So I created a business that intentionally evolved into helping women discover their power, owning who they are, and creating authentic images to support them. Being a leader means listening. Listening to the needs, nurturing the vision, implementing the strategy, and creating impact with integrity. Leadership requires teamwork and collaboration. You can be a leader in many capacities. In my life, I have led within my family by breaking generational curses and in the community by educating, leading by taking action, and standing behind my word.

My work allows others to first envision themselves as the person that they want to be. Helping them to understand that their essence is their light, their purpose and passion is their magic! Helping them to define the soulful capabilities that will provide them with the confidence and clarity to make them strut, ready to lead in their business. I empower them with my camera, helping them to build the confidence and clarity needed to show up as the leader in all aspects of their business. Own their divine makeup, helping them to forge a path to winning.

Ladies, walk boldly, let your light shine bright, and sprinkle your magic everywhere you go. Someone needs your light to bring them out of darkness and your magic to help them transform.

Being a leader means listening. Listening to the needs, nurturing the vision, implementing the strategy, and creating impact with integrity. Leadership requires teamwork and collaboration. You can be a leader in many capacities.

~Leslie M. Gomez

About Leslie M. Gomez

Creative entrepreneur Leslie M. Gomez is an award-winning photographer, motivational speaker, photography educator, and passionate personal brand coach/photographer. She finds joy in helping women create impactful images that support their brand identity, highlighting their superpower so they can make powerful first impressions online.

Leslie is also a registered nurse for more than 16 years; she has been providing compassionate and outstanding healthcare. Over the years, she navigated through the medical ranks, eventually taking on supervisory roles in case management and nursing, specializing in ICU and neuro-trauma.

How did this nurse become a photographer? After receiving a gift of a camera from her husband, Leslie embarked on a new venture that segued into a newfound passion for photography. She first began to master her craft with the intention of capturing the beauty in treasured moments through the filtered lens of sophisticated artistry. Through this platform for creative energy, she provided high-quality portraits with an honest, sincere, and intimate vision. Using her distinctive ability for detail, Leslie began to cultivate her brand as a photographer through the emergence of LMG Photography.

Connect with Leslie:

LMG Photography, LLC

www.IAMLeslieGomez.com

Notes

Chapter 5

Lead with Joy!

Mary Ann Pack

Nothing compares to living in our joy! When we are expressing the joy of who we are, we are in the process of becoming whole - spirit-mind-body. This alignment positively affects everything and everyone around us.

Every belief we hold, every thought we think, every word we say, and every action we take has a ripple effect on the energy of the world. So, if we want to make an impact for good in our world, we must tap into our individual joy embodiment as leaders!

We will be able to do this as we witness the lives of others who are leading the way by example. To me, leadership is all about living out the example of what we want the world to be and receive. If we negate the joy of who *we* are, we will not be nearly as effective in eliciting improvement.

A couple of years ago, I decided to claim the title of joy advocate. This was a bit intimidating because I was initially concerned with what others would think. The more I became aware of who I really was as joy embodied, I couldn't help but claim that title - as should we all!

I believe the purpose of our lives is to experience as much joy as possible (Abraham-Hicks). So, if we're not living in joy, we are not really living our true purpose. They also define success as joy, and I want to be really successful by *that* definition!

Leading with joy is bringing the wholeness of who you are into the present. As a result, you show others the way to BE and offer your life as an example for others to see their *own* possibilities. It's less about *following* a leader and more about walking arm-in-arm in a collaborative effort.

If you utilize a hierarchical style of leadership and the floods of overwhelm or problems arise, you may survive, but those below the floodwaters will drown. You can't be on top of the pile and save very many souls.

When you lead with a heterarchical form of leadership, as in collaborations, your arms are locked together, and you can all float to the surface during the floods of trouble. None are lost in the floodwaters!

As we begin to create wins in our businesses when we are locked arm-in-arm with others, we are rising to the top - together! That's why I love working with collaborations in business. I have so many ideas that I know would be a perfect match for others to join and share their gifts and talents.

That's one reason I started my podcast. I *knew* I wanted to share the stories of transformational leaders. I *knew* the value of sharing how our mess becomes our message. These are messages of hope and possibility!

I also wanted to start my publishing company because I wanted to spread more love and joy in the world. I found a leader who became more of a mentor in Elizabeth Hill as she guided me through the process. Her willingness to lock arms with me allowed me to grow faster than I'd ever imagined, helping me achieve my mission to share love and joy with the world!

Creating my publishing company has enabled me to work with other women who have so much love and joy to share as they write their stories for others to read. Because of the collective collaboration, we are achieving best-selling status for our authors! This can only be accomplished because of the whole, working together as one unit in one fluid movement. We are writing the world happy!

None of this would have happened in my life had I not left the toxic religion in which I was born and raised. I finally had to choose my health and well-being over following leadership that clashed with my soul. Within this religion, so much misogyny kept women down, and I swallowed it hook, line, and sinker for most of my life.

In my mid-40s, I decided to leave and had to *unlearn* so much of the indoctrination that held me back from leading my own life. I had to learn to be the sovereign of my life. I had to choose to lead myself into the love and joy that I am! As I healed, it allowed me to share from my heart and soul and welcome others who were willing to support me. As mentors, coaches, friends, and colleagues walked by my side, we all experienced more love and joy in our healing transformation. This began to prepare me for the world of business pivots that were coming.

In retrospect, I wished I had learned earlier that it's not about competition - it's about complementing one another! Just because someone is in a similar business doesn't mean they are the enemy. Quite the contrary! We are allies, and we can refer clients to each other because of the strengths and gifts we value in each other as we each want to better the world. Our heart-centered mission statements are stronger than our desire to hog any clients that may be better served by a colleague. This attitude stems from a lack consciousness. Not from the expansive abundance of the Universe!

Being more introverted, I've never been a great conversationalist, yet I started a podcast. I never *dreamed* I could host a podcast and interview people, but I have found great joy in doing so! Now, I love interviewing my guests and engaging in meaningful conversations that offer love and joy in every episode.

Yet, I would have never ventured into podcast-land had it not been for mentors who showed me the way and stood by to answer my questions when I was floundering.

Guests have commented that I made it so easy and with a relaxed atmosphere for them to tell their stories. The welcoming space I held for them during the interview made them feel safe and comfortable to share even the most vulnerable experiences. That, right there - fills me with immense joy!

Others who have watched my progress in podcasting have sought my help as they looked forward to starting their own podcast. I love offering any help and guidance that I can. I'm cheering them on to great success!

I've happily walked into the unknown by offering a book anthology for my Unmuted Voices podcast series. I've never collaborated like this before. I simply *knew* that I was being called to share women's stories about how they came to live lives that were unmuted and offer hope to the listeners and readers. All of our voices matter.

In this project, we are laser-focused on living true to our joy and how we're experiencing change and improvement in our lives because of bravely unmuting our voices. And, knowing that I have help in my back pocket when my voice feels shaky doesn't hurt either.

When I work on a collaborative project such as co-authoring a book in my *We Are Joy!* series, I have the foundation of the book in mind, but I want to be open to hearing suggestions and innovative ideas from my co-authors!

For my second book in this series, *Sacred Crystals*, I co-authored with April Goff Brown. In leading the project, I knew the overall value of the book outline and the information I wanted to include, but asking April for her specific input made the work even better! Her expertise and trusted wisdom helped it become a bestseller!

I love people, AND I love my solitude. I've come to believe that everyone needs a time of stillness and solitude to refresh and renew. I would also say that leaders need it even more. Interacting with people can often be very taxing on our energy.

Folks may not intend to present us with challenges but *any* contrast that we experience calls for a time of reflection and going within to choose what we'd prefer to experience the next time. Stillness and solitude allow our minds to quiet and be more receptive to our inner knowledge - our intuition. As our Inner Beings communicate with us through our intuition, we receive downloads for solutions and clarity for action steps.

"If your actions inspire others to dream more, learn more, do more, and become more, you are a leader." ~John Quincy Adams

I know this quote only speaks about our *actions*, but I'm sure the intention is to include *who* we are BEing and *how* we are living out the expression of who we really are. Leading is never only about action. We lead from the wholeness of who we are.

All of life creates a ripple effect. What are we rippling into the world? Is it the vibration of compassion, unity, equanimity, understanding, and encouragement? Is it the vibration of success defined as joy? Are we rippling the waters by locking arms with others so we can rise together?

As I home-educated my sons through high school graduation, I always told them that I expected them to surpass me. Just as I had surpassed my parents' generation, I knew they are to move beyond anything I will do or be in my lifetime.

The same goes for anyone I work with. I want each person I interview, coach in writing, ghostwrite for, or help publish their books to surpass me! I want to live such a beautiful example of love and joy and support that they learn to find and own their successful, joyful, abundant, opulent life! And, I will take joy in each experience of leading them to surpass me and expand the All-That-Is beyond what it is today!

"Every belief we hold, every thought we think, every word we say, and every action we take has a ripple effect on the energy of the world. So, if we want to make an impact for good in our world, we must tap into our individual joy embodiment as leaders!"

~Mary Ann Pack

About Mary Ann Pack

As the publisher at Envision Greatness LLC & Press, Mary Ann Pack shares her love of being a joy advocate! Her background was far from joyful. The religious trauma she suffered affected her relationships, health, finances, and spirituality. Once she began releasing those toxic beliefs and installing new ones that served her well, her life shifted dramatically.

Today, Mary Ann serves others by reminding them who they really are as love and joy embodied. Her mission is to spread more love and joy around the globe, so Envision Greatness Press was born. She began publishing her own book series, *We Are Joy*, that have become best-sellers. Writers work with her to become published authors, maybe for the first time! Her book, *Repurpose & Publish Planner*, is perfect for those who are being called to write a book yet don't have the time to write. Let's write the world happy!

She lives in rural Texas with her husband on their wildlife management area farm.

Connect with Mary Ann:

www.WeAreJoyBooks.com

www.MaryAnnPack.com

www.facebook.com/groups/wearejoybooks

www.linkedin.com/in/maryannpack

www.youtube.com/maryannpack

Notes

Part Two

Culture Shift

Chapter 6

An Emerging Culture of Leadership

Cristal L. Cook, LCSW

It was February 2019, and I was in the beautiful northern Italian town of Aviano, Italy, located at the base of the Dolomite Mountain Range and a mere 90-minutes from the awe-inspiring city of Venice. An hour earlier, I was sitting with friends in the piazza enjoying the beloved local beverage, Prosecco, snacking on potato chips and olives. We were discussing our upcoming travel ideas. One of the benefits of working and living in Europe is that travel is affordable and easy. I loved my European lifestyle and the many benefits of travel, food, and diverse cultures.

Life can change in one hour; it can change a lot. At home, with my head in my hands, I read the disappointing email from my contracting company: sign this new employment contract - the terms of which are horrible - or begin making relocation plans in eight weeks! Neither option is appealing, so what else is there to do but turn this situation into an opportunity?

As much as I loved living in Italy and working with the teens at the school on the military base, I knew that, professionally, I was stagnant. I had been working as an Adolescent Support and Counseling Services (ASACS) Counselor in Germany and Italy for the past seven years. While I had been an informal leader in the mental health field amongst my colleagues and peers for the past

20 years, I had never been in a formal leadership position; I enjoyed the client interaction too much. It now made sense to change that. The supervisory position, Program Manager and Clinical Supervisor for the United States Air Force Europe's (USAFE) ASACS program was mine if I wanted it. So, I accepted the challenge and learned, stretched, faced many unexpected challenges, and grew in ways I never imagined.

Once I got on board, I was handed a brand-new staff – all were new to the ASACS program, new to living overseas, and new to working with the military. In my first month, I was informed that the Air Force was looking to kill the contract: the new team and I would be sent back to the States, jobless. I worked tirelessly with my Air Force leadership to keep the program going and the jobs of my team intact, then COVID-19 hit and the world went into lockdown. Challenge after challenge made my new role a difficult one at times, but difficult lessons are often the best.

New to "official" leadership, I read everything I could find on the topic. I wanted to be the best leader possible - not one consumed with power, but the leader that I always wanted - a leader that supported and took care of their team and inspired people to reach their full potential. Simon Sinek brilliantly captures this in his quote, "Leadership is not about being in charge. Leadership is about taking care of those in your charge."

Leadership styles have changed over the years for the better! Early in my career, supervisors led with fear and intimidation as the motivator, and fostered internal competition. The feeling of shame is damaging, and most will do anything to avoid it. This style of leadership creates a culture of fear and distrust. When mistakes are made, the tendency is to hide them rather than fix them. People don't feel safe presenting new ideas, thinking outside of the box, or growing into their full potential, and working collectively as a team is riddled with competitive barriers.

Growth is not accomplished without trial, error, and mistakes - the fear of punishment squashes potential growth.

Take, for example, the 3M Corporation, whose culture encourages collaboration, individual innovation, and has a high tolerance for mistakes without pressure for short-term results. This type of environment fosters creativity without fear of punishment, hence the creation of the popular Post-it Notes. Dr. Spencer Silver, a 3M scientist, was working to discover a strong adhesive, but he accidentally created the opposite: a very light-sticking adhesive that easily peeled away from all surfaces. Even though this was not his goal, he believed that it could somehow be useful, so he shared this "failed" discovery with colleagues hoping someone would have an idea for this new creation.

A few years later, a fellow 3M scientist, Art Fry, found a use for Dr. Silver's invention. While practicing with his church choir, Mr. Fry had been using scraps of paper to bookmark the hymns; however, these pieces of paper inevitably fell out of the hymnbook. What he needed was a light adhesive to mark the pages. Mr. Fry and Dr. Silver collaborated in the lab and put the light adhesive on small squares of paper to create the popular and useful Post-it Note.[1] Remove fear of punishment, and internal competition, and magic can happen!

The old style of leadership of fear is simply not tolerated by our younger generations, forcing positive change. Effective leadership has evolved into the "servant-leader": supportive and caring, with a focus on mentorship, assistance, inspiration, and motivation, a style where we pick people up, help them become the best version of themselves, shine the light on their strengths and help them to develop in areas where they are challenged.

---

[1] 3M (2022). *History Timeline: Post-it® Notes.*
https://www.post-it.com/3M/en_US/post-it/contact-us/about-us/

One of the most powerful lessons I learned as the Clinical Supervisor surprised me completely: employees come to the job with their own wounds from their past. Although I was nothing like the parents, teachers, coaches, family members, or former supervisors who had caused them pain, the mere commonality of being in a perceived position of power and authority triggered those wounds. I learned that being present and aware of the patterns of how my team members reacted to me as a leader helped me to understand how their wounds are triggered. I learned to proceed in a manner that did not dig into those wounds but soothed them.

The reactions prompted by this triggering can be confusing and frustrating. This topic was not covered in the numerous books I read about leadership, so it came as a complete surprise. It took some time to understand what was happening when team members reacted in a way that simply did not make sense to me. Reactions ranged from rage over the lack of control over computer issues, to the avoidance of asking questions, to absolute fear over very small issues and mistakes, to lack of ownership of mistakes, to lack of teamwork and collaboration, to shutting down emotionally when treated harshly by clients' parents and other providers (a given in our profession).

Having a team helped me to gain perspective, as each person's wounded reaction was out of the norm and different from the other team members' responses to the exact same situation. It was important for me to stay grounded and not react emotionally, even when I felt frustrated. I found it helpful to remind the team that everyone makes mistakes that can be used as learning opportunities and that we then do our best to resolve them. Providing reassurance, boundaries, guidance, and expectations in a calm and consistent manner was vital.

I don't believe that it is important for us to find the root of that wounding, as we are not their therapists, but it is important to be aware that we, in a position of leadership, may trigger a wounding and to notice the pattern. I will be completely honest: there were times I felt highly aggravated, but my role as the leader was to keep those emotions in check and treat my team with respect while providing helpful guidance. I love how Richard Branson captures this sentiment in his quote, "Great things can be achieved by leading through wisdom, empathy, and integrity – with no other agenda than humanity."

Another lesson I learned is the importance of a highly selective and rigorous hiring process so that the team is the right fit for the organization. This should include thoroughly reviewing resumes, talking to prior employers and co-workers, and conducting interviews with a specific rubric and a personality profile to ensure that the person's values and motivations will match the culture of the organization. A personality profile is an invaluable resource to leadership as it conveys the person's strengths, work, and communication styles. Some companies utilize the NEO Personality Inventory assessment for prospective and current employees. I am trained and certified in performing these assessments, and the information gleaned from them is incredibly useful in selecting the right team and in better understanding the team you currently have.

Once the candidate is selected as a potential employee, it is imperative that the person understands and is excited about the organization's vision – the Why. When people are working towards something bigger than themselves, and for a vision that they believe in, there is instant motivation. The skills and other details can be taught.

When I stepped into the role as the ASACS Clinical Supervisor, an entirely new staff had been recently hired, with a very low standard for selection. The criteria simply consisted of two questions: "Are you a Licensed Clinical Social Worker (LCSW)?" and "Do you want to live and work in Europe?" The team was excited to live in Europe and had no concept of the program's vision.

What I learned is that I needed to immediately "sell" the vision and ASACS mission to ensure their buy-in. Simply explaining the program's purpose, scope, expectations, the day-to-day activities, history, and policies were not enough for my team to be inspired by the Why. It was up to me to make the vision clear and inspiring. Eventually, I did learn this missing piece and worked to create trainings so that the team would all be working with a clearer vision and a more synergistic and collaborative approach.

Fast forward three years, to the spring of 2022, after nine years of living and working overseas, the last three in western Germany - I'm in the midst of taking another leap: I will be leaving my position as Clinical Supervisor/Program Manager to relocate back to the States. I am becoming an entrepreneur! I have written the Crystalline Vibes children's book series (the first book in the series will be released in 2022), as well as providing NEO assessments to coaches, individuals, and managers, providing transformational coaching services, and offering workshops and retreats. With the freedom of not being in a position of middle management with a large organization, I have the ability to create my company and a team in a way that represents my values, brand, and vision: To Raise the Vibration of the Planet, One Person at a Time.

While it is time for me to pass the baton to a new manager, it is bittersweet. I have experienced tremendous growth as a leader, and as a person, in the past few years, and I am grateful for all of the difficult lessons along the way. My path was riddled with many lessons but also with a deep connection with my team. I am grateful for the trust extended to me, demonstrated by the vulnerability each person shared; I honor that. As Brene Brown's research shows, connection cannot happen without vulnerability, and trust must be present for vulnerability.[2]

During our journey together, I hope my team felt protected, supported, and pushed to be the best versions of themselves. I mostly hope that they truly felt that I always had their backs, as bullies continue to exist in the workplace and find their way into positions of power and authority. A quality that helped me in this area is an almost unhealthy lack of fear which allowed me the courage to do what I believed was in the best interest of my team, no matter what. That made making tough decisions actually quite easy.

Moving into entrepreneurship, I am currently leading a team of remarkable women that are total game-changers on this journey. This team approach is absolutely a heterarchical one, with teamwork and collaboration that is creating sheer magic. I had the privilege of hand-picking each person, and they were mutually selective about choosing to work with me. Our synergistic collaboration is nothing short of miraculous!

Our individual missions resonate, and as a collective group, our passions for our missions have created a fireball of unstoppable energy. It's like nothing I have ever experienced! In a few short months, working via email and Zoom in various time zones, we quickly recognized each person's superpowers, which allowed for efficiency and top-quality performance. We work like a well-oiled machine, which was incredible to witness, especially when faced with deadlines. This type of synergy is often not achieved with a team, ever.

What I have learned from these two very different leadership

---

[2] Brown, B. (2012). *The Power of Vulnerability: Teachings on Authenticity, Connection and Courage.* Sounds True.

experiences is that when all parties involved are passionate about an organization's vision/mission before joining the team, the momentum, energy, and collaboration are instantly present. When one is required to sell the Why to an already formed team, there is a tremendous amount of time and energy devoted to convincing others of the importance of the mission, and the team may or may not ever be inspired by the Why. When everyone believes in and is motivated by, the Why from the very beginning, stand back and watch the magic begin!

I believe that as we embrace feminine energy while holding positions of leadership, people will feel inspired and safe, and creativity will increase. The days of competition-at-all-costs, both within and outside of our organizations, will diminish. Rather than trying to squash our competition, we will collaborate, share resources and ideas, pull each other along, and learn from each other.

We need to get to a place where, as humans, we aren't trying to take the entire pie for ourselves but realize that there is an endless supply of pies waiting to come out of the oven. Working synergistically, rather than competitively, has the power to help humanity reach new potential that will change the world. That, my friends, is raising the vibration of the planet one person at a time - my personal Why!

"Effective leadership has evolved into the "servant-leader": supportive and caring, with a focus on mentorship, assistance, inspiration, and motivation, a style where we pick people up, help them become the best version of themselves, shine the light on their strengths, and help them to develop in areas where they are challenged."

~Cristal L. Cook, LCSW

About Cristal L. Cook, LCSW

Cristal Lynn Cook, LCSW, grew up in Mancos, Colorado, population 1000. At a young age, Cristal had a passion for rescuing animals, creating adventures, and helping the underdog. Her journey to grown-up-hood took a meandering path that involved several career paths from CPA to FBI agent and ultimately to finding her true calling as a licensed clinical social worker (LCSW).

The broad field of Social Work was the answer to Cristal's curious, joyful nature, and for the past 20 years she found it incredibly rewarding working with children, adolescents, and families as a therapist and advocate. Her adventurous spirit was satisfied as she traveled internationally doing what she loves: helping teens and families, rescuing animals, and exploring the world.

Connect with Cristal:

www.OperationTransformationBooks.com

www.facebooks.com/operationtransformationbooks

www.instagram.com/operationtransformationbooks

www.linkedin.com/in/cristalcook

Notes

Chapter 7

Leading with IMPACT

Amy Flores-Young

Growing up during the street light curfew generation in the Northeast United States, I was a very independent child. Big ideas, creative solutions, being a helper, and going for it seemed innate to me. At least, that is how I recall it. I was also the little sister who laid in the street so her brother and friends could jump over me with their BMX bikes. Yes, that's one of the few concussions from my youth. So maybe add a risk taker.

I was bold, observant, and thoughtfully earnest. I was not the loudest, but I never shied away from sharing an opinion. These verbalizations were not always well received, but I was lucky that I was not made to feel small for them either. Thank you, Mom and Dad - I had no idea what a gift that was until hearing opposite experiences from so many of my peers. I don't feel that I stepped into leadership. More like launched into it, as I was comfortable with risk.

I was a "Y rat" - the term of endearment for the middle school and high school kids who were constantly hanging out at the YMCA. I never got why it was "rat," but now, as an adult, as I sit here, I see how we scurried from corner to corner of the building and took over (infested) any area we were in. NOW, I get it! The YMCA has two national teen programs; Youth and Government™ and Leaders Club. At that time, you had to be in high school to participate. As a proud rat, I anxiously awaited my freshman year. Not to "be" in high school and all the other rights of passage but to

FINALLY be able to get into those programs. I could not wait to have a forum to nurture my strengths and cultivate my weaknesses. Of course, I didn't consciously realize this as an adolescent. I just wanted to be where the fun was and be able to volunteer behind the front desk for my service hours.

My participation in those programs was life-altering. My father passed away while I was in high school, and it was my fellow Leaders that rode it out with me and never expected me to be anything other than myself in all my grief, goofiness, and teen angst. Throughout those years, I was given the room to safely fail and learn from it with the reflective support of advisors in the programs. The cornerstone of my identity was so firmly rooted in the YMCA that in college, I changed majors (senior year!) from medical technology to sociology so I could transition directly into a full-time career as a YMCA Director.

I was a get-stuff-done doer. Quick to take action, offer the solutions, a fixer. These are some of the new/young blood traits that made me stand out. I quickly moved up the organizational chart taking leadership over programs, and becoming a Senior Director in my twenties.

When looking at the difference between hierarchy and heterarchy and how it related to my leadership, there was one big lesson I learned early on in this professional role. I was promoted to supervise an evening youth club that was mostly attended by at-risk youth working to stay out of trouble. It was well established and staffed by people older than me, who had been there for years. I was clearly the LEADER, though. I had so many ideas that would grow the program, save the budget, and serve the youth "better."

Needless to say, when I announced these new ways of doing things, it landed like a lead balloon. The tension was palpable for weeks, and I quickly understood the term "backlash" in a professional sense. While the ideas and the changes were not all bad, it was the way they were communicated. I did not take into consideration the value of the institutional knowledge I had in my staff. Nor did I ask the participants what they wanted and how they wanted to be supported.

Once I offered the open forum for these discussions and took responsibility for my impulsive leadership, things improved. There was an open door for feedback, ideas, change, and collaboration. Administration, staff, and participants all had a shared, clear goal and understanding of what they brought to the table to make it a success.

I look back at my YMCA career with such fondness and immense gratitude that I was given the opportunity to learn the benefits and importance of constant collaboration. While I always worked collaboratively with other departments, other community agencies, parents and families, city services, and our direct vendors, I didn't realize how unique that is compared to so many other industries.

I worked for a total of four different YMCAs during my decade-long career. I enjoyed all my time there, all the people I was fortunate enough to work with, and those who allowed me to serve them. A life-long career at the YMCA was my (youthful) dream come true.

Sadly, once I became a parent of a disabled child, I could not keep up with the 'all-hours' schedule of a YMCA position, and my passion shifted from community youth work toward disability rights and advocacy.

I did not know what the heterarchy structure was until Elizabeth Hill and Dr. Davia Shepherd approached me about THIS collaboration. While thinking about which parts of my story to share, it became crystal clear that in every role I have been in, I fought the hierarchical model and tried to make it heterarchical.

I have been an educational advocate for my children and

many others. There is a "team meeting," but it is usually an us versus them model of the administration versus the family. Bridging communications and finding common values for outcomes was always my approach.

I have participated on many task forces, boards, and policy change groups. This work has always frustrated me because the gears of change moved so slowly. Working to bring various resources together was disheartening, as so much was siloed with no lines of collaboration. Needless to say, I didn't stay in these arenas for more than a few years at a time.

In another instance, I was hired to oversee a state grant program that was centered around bringing community collaborators into after-school support programs in the public schools. This position came to me as I was the person outside of the system, with all the community connections. The job description was written in all collaborative terms. Being led in the uber hierarchical structure of the public schools, let's just say we did not have the same definition of collaboration. I only lasted one grant cycle.

These are just some examples. I didn't understand the burn-out I had and lack of fulfillment in many of these roles until thinking about it in hierarchy versus heterarchy terms. I was doing good work. Community organizing towards change. Impacting systems at the local, state, and national level. Why did I feel so useless and empty? There was no shared support or real, sustainable goal. Mostly reactive and not proactive.

When asked what top three words describe you? "Leader" usually comes up somewhere. I now know that I need to specify "collaborative leader" or "heterarchical leader" if I have the time to explain the word. This is a distinction that needs more attention. There needs to be a paradigm shift in what leadership looks like. A shift in how business is done and what is considered successful.

We often say collaboration over competition and focus on abundance, that there is enough for everyone. It is time to make these normalized thoughts. No, not thought, but belief.

While I was advancing my career in service, wondering what would be next, that choice was made for me. I had to step away from my career and transition home to be a full-time caregiver. That is a deeper dive story for another time. After the novelty of being home wore off, and the reality of caregiving crept in, I realized too much of my identity was tied to my position - my hierarchical role. I took the opportunity of this transition time to determine WHO I wanted to be and what I wanted to create.

I have always loved the zen of completing puzzles. Sorting all the little pieces knowing the big beautiful design it will form. Trial and error, seeing it all come together. Sometimes the process would flow. Sometimes there would be long moments of frustration when I couldn't see how anything fit. How I got to the place of becoming a soul-aligned entrepreneur was not linear. Reflecting on these past experiences, I now see all the pieces of the puzzle and how they fit together into the business, I have now that gets me excited every day.

Sure, I was competent with this and that, I may even enjoy it, but could I build a business on it? Understanding the difference between what I could do versus what I wanted to do was harder to figure out than I thought it would be. It was also very clear what I didn't want to do and who I wanted to work with. I read the build your business-type books and did the exercises in them. I journaled, let it sit, and came back to see what kept rising to the top. I also reached out to tons of small business people and entrepreneurs. I didn't do it on my own. I built a trusted network around me for support.

I actually cried the day it all came together; I could see it so clearly. It was a simple recipe of everything I wanted to include.

Travel + Business Strategy + Collaboration = Retreats. Travel is always transformational and collaborative, creating a deeper understanding in the world around us and of ourselves! Travel was a priority for my family, and it is those shared experiences that built the best parts of our relationships. Business strategy isn't goals and metrics. It is seeing the bigger picture, as well as the details to get there. Within a business strategy, you need to determine the ways to work smarter, not harder, and how to manage your leadership energy. This is something I am very attuned to and very good at guiding others on.

Collaboration is my favorite part of what I do. When I first started this work, I felt it was more of a backend collaboration. Working with me allowed the leader to be spotlighted and shine while I was doing the details in the background. As I have grown my transformational travel strategist business, I have stepped into my magic as a true partner, not a background supporter.

You may think that the pandemic would have decimated my travel-based business. Did I forget to mention that I am the eternal optimist? By no means do I wish to minimize the effects of the pandemic or the two years; my bottom line was bright red.

The pandemic has been the perfect opportunity to cultivate collaborations in the most creative way. Through increased virtual networking opportunities, my community grew by 600%. Being able to stand firm that I would not pivot to virtual events made me stand out as a thought leader in the retreat planning space. I was able to build relationships that have led to power partnerships and wonderful friendships throughout the world. Within the pandemic pause, I was able to find my niche, build out my brand, and call in the audience and partners that align with my service.

A special shout-out to M. Shannon Hernandez and Amy Hager of the Joyful Business Revolution™ for their constant support, coaching, and role modeling on how to build a business with clarifying messaging and more joy!

To be clear, I don't lead retreats. I partner with coaches and thought leaders to increase their impact and income with intention, through them incorporating retreats into their business. Ensuring that these transformative experiences are aligned with the participant's outcomes, the unique vision, the leader's energy, delivery style, and brand. Using my signature I.M.P.A.C.T. model, we build out events that help these business owners create powerful retreats that make them money that they can actually enjoy while creating a memorable experience that turns their guests into raving fans.

The I.M.P.A.C.T. model was another bonus outcome of the partnerships gained over the pandemic. It is the foundation of how I work with clients at all levels in my business.

Intention – Create your unique vision that keeps your clients at the center of the experience and aligns with your desired outcomes.

Method – Map out your logistics, agenda, and activities to meet your objectives and create a powerful impact.

Profit - Fill in my formulated budget to ensure the event is priced for profit and reflects the value you provide.

Action Plan – Ongoing accountability and timelines, including a detailed on-site game plan and everything you need to bring your A-Game.

Customer Experience – We look at the entire client journey from initial brand contact through becoming a loyal paying client.

Take Away – How do you want people to leave your event, and what outcome and experience do you want them to be talking about?

Throughout the I.M.P.A.C.T. process, in partnership, I support you so you can collaborate and reach your clients more effectively. It's a full heterarchy circle and brings me so much joy! Why are so many people OK with associating their work with thoughts like hustle, daily grind, and the rat race? My thoughts around work are ease, flow, joyful, streamline, and friends.

When I started my non-profit career, I thought changing the world had to happen from the large systems; a top-down policy approach. I now know that powerful change that can cause societal disruption comes from the individual outward. The ripple effect is the ripple effect because it is a simple visual that all can understand. Keeping that visual top-of-mind is how I increase the impact of the clients I work with.

Regardless of the magic you bring in working with clients, there is ALWAYS a transformation in the outcome. YOU are the water in the container waiting for the clients to jump in. Are they a small one-to-one ripple - think a gravel stone? Maybe you do a small group, and it is a handful of gravel stones, and the ripples overlap a little. But stones sink, and the ripple fades.

The transformational effect is intensified when working in person, during a shared group experience without distractions, where the inertia of the transformation is not stuttered with time between sessions. That is like throwing a dozen baseballs into a pool where the ripples overlap as the balls are supported. As they bump off each other, more ripples come into play. If you can float twelve baseballs, why not twenty, forty, one hundred? THAT is increasing your IMPACT!

Remember when I mentioned in the beginning that more businesses need to BELIEVE in the concept of collaboration over competition? Well, I believe it. I often reach out to other retreat leaders and planners to ask about locations. We even refer clients to each other if we feel they are a better fit. I swap training and speaking opportunities with other thought leaders to activate creativity in other audiences. Planting the seeds that playing bigger does not mean working harder.

I promote my client's programs and retreats, as well as others, because that is how we get more ripples. I share stories in anthology books like this one. Over a two-year pandemic frozen travel industry, I doubled my revenue while decreasing the actual hours I worked! Slow down and read that again. That type of growth is only possible through collaboration - where all players are on the same level. No one is better or more important than the other. Resources are shared regardless of credit given.

Leading collaboratively, where we all help each other grow, has helped my business soar. I know it can for you too.

"Why are so many people OK with associating their work with thoughts like hustle, daily grind, and the rat race? My thoughts around work are ease, flow, joyful, streamline, and friends."

~Amy Flores-Young

About Amy Flores-Young

Transformational Travel Strategist and Retreat Concierge Amy Flores-Young (Flo-Yo) specializes in bringing your dream retreats to life, helping you reclaim joy in traveling. With her signature IMPACT system, she partners with coaches and leaders to build profitable and powerful in-person experiences that leave everyone with memories for a lifetime.

Amy has perfected the art of weaving together the ultimate location and itinerary that both engages and energizes your guests. All while fiercely holding your intention and aligning to your brand. She is a sought-after speaker in the world of travel planning and retreat business strategy, and when she is not planning and traveling, she is petting every puppy she meets, DJing kitchen dance parties, and shopping for new hoodies.

Connect with Amy:

www.FloYoTravel.com

www.linkedin.com/in/amy-floyo

Notes

Chapter 8

Heart-Led Leadership

Rosemary King

Leadership has always been a part of my life. Whether that was to be a mediator for friends and family or to protect others, I have always found myself in situations where compassion was necessary for the process of moving forward.

In-your-face motivational speakers or business innovators often excel at being loud and obnoxious rather than exemplifying cooperation and collaboration in their fields. Their presence in the business sector is hailed as strong and successful, and while they are successful in their own rights, their cutthroat antics are not an approach that I feel best encompasses heart-led leadership. Even I fell into this trap of being overly aggressive with some of my approaches to leading others. It takes time and willingness to change your ways when you've recognized mistakes made; to do and be better.

Leadership also doesn't mean having to run into a battlefield and fight. Although those types of situations frequently occur, I can't help but wonder if we looked at leadership from a compassionate entity rather than as something that is disruptive in nature.

Leadership is about being a safe space for those that are behind your cause, so they feel free to voice concerns without fear of being gaslighted or called names because of a difference of opinions. Leading needs to make space for growth and confidence for all parties so that they can evolve into better people and create stronger communities.

Leadership & My Past

I've always felt called to lead. Even as a child, I looked to do more, to be someone that helped. Leaders to me were helpers and doers. I remember in grade school, some of my classmates were making fun of someone on our bus, and I stood up and told them to stop being mean and then sat in his seat so no one else could bother him.

When I entered high school, I had to decide on what I was going to do with my life and where. I decided that the military was the way to go. My grandfathers served in World War II. My grandmothers served in nursing capacities. Turns out that helping people is in my blood. I joined the Army JROTC at my high school, so I could learn about leadership.

In everything I do, I put in the effort and time to do the skillset well. And if I know I'm not up to the task, rather than trying to force myself into something that isn't right or doesn't fit, I walk away knowing I gave it my all. What I have learned from leadership is that there will always be favoritism from those higher up and that sometimes those that are leaders should never be put in that position. Not all leaders are created equal, and when push comes to shove, good leaders know when and how to compromise, be respectful and take a step back and let their pride take a hit.

When I was in high school, I worked my tail off to do well in JROTC. It wasn't hard or challenging work. Simply needed to follow instructions. But at the end of the day, when my time was coming up for more advanced positions and moving up the "chain of command," I learned a hard lesson. Leaders are human. They are not gods. Nor are they all-knowing. Revolutionary, right? But when you think of military leaders, they're placed in some of the toughest situations someone will ever have to face in their lifetime. And those decisions are made to the best of their abilities, with the knowledge on hand, prejudices, and all.

This can lead to inadequacies and keeping the circle of influence like those that are most like you. While this could be good, it presents problems because for lack of not only diversity but also a lack of choice and support for those that are under you. Being a resolute leader means intentionally surrounding yourself with people that have diverse opinions, that are otherwise contrasting to your own so that you can receive constructive and differentiated feedback rather than in an echo chamber.

I can't tell you how often my perception has been wrong based on knowledge known but lack of knowledge given. Not knowing the whole story and making assumptions can lead to some disastrous results.

One example is when I was frustrated at the lack of participation from others in a service group I was a part of. I thought it meant that they were lazy or didn't care, and that was the furthest from the truth. They were dedicated to other responsibilities that had priority in their life, but I was too blinded to see that, which led to misunderstanding, and selfishly I would call them out for "poor behavior" to have them "buck up." Unfortunately, they walked away from a program that was meant to be supportive for them and their families. Instead, my arrogance turned on them when they needed someone to care the most.

Volunteering as a Teen vs. Adult

Mr. Rogers said it best, "All we're ever asked to do in this life is to treat our neighbor — especially our neighbor who is in need — exactly as we would hope to be treated ourselves. That's our ultimate responsibility." I try to live by this simple explanation of the Golden Rule every day.

When I volunteered as a teen, I took direction from the adults around me. Sometimes I would push an issue, specifically if I felt like the decision was being used as punishment over one or two bad decisions by a couple of people and not considering the entire group's behavior. It didn't work all the time, but at least my friends knew I would stand up for what we thought was right rather than just allowing it to happen without a discussion.

When I volunteered to be a moderator of a pregnancy chat board, I did my very best to do what was right for the members of the community. Having developed strong personal relationships with these individuals who were pregnant meant that I and other moderators had a firsthand account of what was working and not working. Yet our voices were silenced when a new company purchased the website and wanted to overhaul the experience for members.

It was very abrasive, with a lot of in-fighting between moderators and administrators of the new parent company. I was fired from that position because of my pushback; even with the support of others, I was made an example of because the parent company didn't want insubordination. The whole situation was eye-opening in how not to lead. Leaders should never go into a situation as the new person and destroy the foundation that was built before them. Learn from the membership, volunteers, and workers, and then after a period of discovery, go in with small and meaningful changes. Otherwise, you'll cause more harm than good, and you'll be left picking up pieces that shouldn't have been broken in the first place.

As far as I know, that parent company eventually kept things as is, took some of my ideas and used them as their own, and didn't change much of anything at the end of the day. What a wasted opportunity for those that wanted to make things better for members of that community, all because of someone's ego.

When my children were part of a youth program over a decade ago, I volunteered, first as a youth leader and as a committee member. Then moving up the ranks to serving as the chair, as well as other positions, because there were more roles than adults to serve.

Sometimes I would be firm and combative in my approach when dealing with others, especially if I felt like they weren't pulling their weight or making promises they couldn't keep. Those times, I failed as a leader. Instead of recognizing their need for help, I cut them off and threw it in their face that I thought they were not doing a good enough job. When they only needed a safe space to share their worries without judgment or fear of retribution.

This experience highlighted my poor habits, and I realized I was not a good leader because of my destructive actions against other adults in the program. What is even crazier, is that I was awarded for my leadership in that organization. Not once, but twice. Due to some of the strides made by myself and others with the youth program. Taking time setting up events, spreading the word of its existence, setting up community awareness, fundraising so that we could provide for all the kids that needed it, their program fees paid for by us, volunteer opportunities, and having an agenda that provided all the elements for the youth advancement. And yet, through all of this, I felt like my recognition was a reinforcement of my poor leadership. Instead, my leadership should not have been praised; however, as I pointed out earlier, some form of militant style of leadership is what people recognize as quality leadership.

Today, I do my best to use the structure of hierarchy (as it is the structure of the organizations I'm a volunteer of) and sprinkle it with cooperation and collaboration, always trying to not balance but harmonize the qualities of others to the best of my ability.

When the opportunity comes up to make tough decisions, I will allow others the opportunity to share their thoughts, and that gives me better perspectives on how to handle a situation.

Parenthood & Leadership

Does being a parent make you a leader? I think on some level, yes, all parents are leaders to their children, whether they realize this or not. Being able to guide your child in the direction of good ethical behavior and compassion towards others is important. When I was a child, we volunteered as a family in our church. I remember helping with the summer festival and spaghetti dinners or helping with the band boosters. I enjoyed those times. Having my parents show the importance of giving back is something I made sure I passed along to my six kids.

When I became a mother, I didn't think of my role as a "leader," and yet, as mothers, we are. Mothers are often the person that their children look up to. I have tried my best to be a good leader for my children, but even with the best intentions, unintended consequences can happen.

When my kids were younger, we did the whole hierarchy, "because I said so" line was repeated, and there was no room for concessions. Though I did try to parent more with my heart, with an attachment approach, I struggled to find a balance that worked well for my children and me. Now that I have found my groove, I wish I could go back and re-do their childhood. Knowing what I know now, I would have opted to handle situations differently. But that is neither here nor there, and all I can do is do better in the future. You see, every opportunity to lead has given me new lessons on what an impactful and compassionate leader should look like.

Leadership & My Business

In my business, Heart-Led Concierge, I work as a personal assistant service provider specializing in decluttering and organization. I want my clients to feel accepted and encouraged. To do this, I wanted to give my clients a safe place to navigate their clutter without feeling embarrassed or judged. And while I know some clients don't need that approach, many do.

By being present with my clients, I have been able to give them a platform to transform their lives, one stepping stone at a time. It's slow-moving and doesn't always work for others. Sometimes, it can be hard to picture the end result when things aren't going as fast as you'd like them to go. One thing I've learned about chronic disorganization is that if you go too fast, you'll trip yourself up trying to get there, resulting in a lack of progress.

While I mostly work with people that have chronic disorganization, and it might not seem like decluttering your home can grow an individual in leadership, it does allow for the individual to own their decisions, good or bad, and offer a safe space for them to try new things without fear of judgment. If something doesn't work, no worries, we try something else. Because clutter, especially if it's due to a response to trauma, may provoke unpleasant emotional responses.

Having compassionate support and a gentleness approach to the situation at hand provides an opportunity for growth that isn't seen in other decluttering approaches. There can be a harshness when clearing clutter using a ridged system, especially if that system ignores the trauma. By being more heart-centered in my approach, clients are given adequate space for personal growth and support that is generally not provided in similar businesses.

Leadership Evolving

Over the past decade, I have come to the realization that people only want to be treated well and heard. They're already under enormous stress, and their role as an employee or volunteer, or other subordinate role doesn't diminish their ability to serve as well as they are capable of. It is through this realization that I've tried to re-evaluate my methodology in leadership, and I hope that the evolution of my leadership continues to evolve over time. For without evolution, I will not be able to truly be a great leader.

What I need to be mindful of moving forward is that even though some people may be wary of the approach to leadership with compassion and collaboration, over time their concerns may reduce as they are participating in different opportunities more than before.

I know that change can be difficult. People give up too soon, or they fear that they're making the wrong choice, so they pass the buck of responsibility for any fallout. They may fear the backlash or harsh reaction from others if it doesn't work out. They may feel that they're incapable of putting skin in the game or doing what is necessary for success because failure isn't an option. That shouldn't define who they are, and good leaders should offer up solutions on how to properly handle stressful situations. A good leader will walk alongside their colleague, lending support and a listening ear so a positive decision can be made.

Unfortunately, if this doesn't happen, then those in positions of minor leadership roles may give themselves an excuse and way out of a situation that they couldn't handle. It is that kind of thinking and harsh criticism that hinders the advancement of subordinates and stunts their growth as a leader.

Being a leader also means being responsible for mistakes and taking corrective action so as not to repeat those mistakes again.

To be willing to apologize, even if it causes you to lose your position. To own your mistakes means you're mature enough to learn from them rather than deflecting responsibility and placing blame on others. Courageous leaders lead with integrity.

Passive participation also isn't the answer to being a leader. Taking no action can lead to undesirable results. Fear of failure can make even the best leaders fail. Similarly, when a leader does something that could be seen as a mistake or disruptive, it's important not to first react with an iron fist but to gently encourage dialogue to determine what and why something happened the way it did. Was it due to the inability to complete the task at hand? Was it due to a lack of desire to do the job? Was it because there was little to no guidance? All these things can add up and cause problems if not addressed in an open and transparent way.

Maybe the person really is a jerk and doesn't have the resources to voice their concerns constructively. But perhaps, they're reacting the only way they were taught. In those moments, it's best to step back and assess, then evaluate and conclude on how to proceed.

Being a leader is more than overseeing people, businesses, or organizations. Leading means you are taking active steps to grow, mentor, and support those around you to the best of your ability. Sometimes that means you must make those executive decisions. And sometimes, it means you get to help someone out of their comfort zone and watch them fly.

It's okay for people to feel unsure about their capabilities; if they have positive accountability and support from their peers, they can grow and thrive in whatever environment they're in. When we invest in others' success, we will have a genuine impact on ourselves and on the lives of others in our community.

"When we invest in others' success, we will have a genuine impact on ourselves and on the lives of others in our community."

~Rosemary King

About Rosemary King

Rosemary King is the owner of Heart-Led Concierge, a personal assistant service provider specializing in decluttering and organizing support in-person and virtually. She is active in her community and volunteers for several organizations. She has a degree in Psychology, is a Master Reiki Practitioner, and is working on other certifications to assist her with her clients.

She is married to Wayne, and they have six children spanning from ages 13-22 years old. Her family enjoys hiking, camping, and antiquing together. They also have a German Shepherd named Savannah and a pet ferret named Minka.

Connect with Rosemary:

www.HeartLedConcierge.com

support@heartledconcierge.com

www.facebook.com/heartledconcierge

www.instagram.com/heartledconcierge

www.pinterest.com/heartledconcierge

Notes

Part Three

A New Organizational Paradigm

Chapter 9

Cultivating Your Collaborative Team

Shawniel Chamanlal, LCSW

Being a leader has always been an innate feeling for me. From the time I was young and began working in a bank, I *knew* that I was meant to be in leadership. I recognized what worked and what didn't work within the leadership at the bank.

I knew micromanaging was not for me because I had watched the dynamics playing out in relationships with people when they were exposed to micromanagement. I knew I wanted my leadership to be more heart-centered and authentic. As I moved up at the bank, I had the opportunity to shine as a supervisor, and my boss cried when I left.

It was time to move into another area of business, and I became a licensed clinical social worker. During graduate school, I began to hold the vision of cultivating other therapists. So many therapists only wanted to work for mental health agencies, and they thought I was a bit crazy because I wanted my own private practice. I knew I wanted to have a collective group of healers and helpers.

Taking advantage of the stepping stones of working at agencies helped me understand the inner workings of the business. Yet, so many of the managers were ill-equipped to lead, or they were micromanagers. They weren't heart-centered, and I simply didn't align with this style of leadership.

It did, however, give me the opportunity to fine-tune what I wanted for my team and myself. So, in 2018, I finally built up the confidence, and with a push from my spiritual business coach, I decided it was time to open my agency. I created the platform on which I would build my agency - under my unique, heart-centered, authentic style of leadership.

I created a vision board of sorts of what I wanted my business to look like. It was a template of what I wanted and who I wanted on my team.

By 2020 with the demand from mental health issues and the pandemic, I was ready to hire my first team member. She was a graduate school colleague who believed in me when I told others that I wanted my own group practice!

I now have ten therapists because everything has aligned! Almost everything that I looked for, if not better in regard to staffing, came into my reality. I made sure to infuse everything that our team does, emphasizing self-care. As our team members demonstrate self-care, our clients also benefit.

Autonomy and independence are also important factors as I wanted to create a safe space for my therapists to express what they needed - whether issues or sharing wins. Because I've set these boundaries and with my leadership style, I just keep attracting people that are aligned with the practice, and it's so fulfilling.

When I interview people, I always ask them what they want. How do they see their practice within the agency? What are their ideal schedule and client load? This helps them discover their autonomy and independence. When you work in other agencies or community health centers, you don't have many choices about your schedule, type of clients, or being innovative. But, in my practice, I want my team to have choices - this isn't a dictatorship. This is a collaboration where we all have input and are heard and seen as valuable members.

The skills I learned during my years in banking helped me realize how delegating was a good leadership practice. I feel that this has allowed me to help others learn new skills and build competence and confidence to progress in their own leadership skills. As my team members want more responsibility, I'm able to help them become better leaders and managers. Then, they learn to be autonomous and independent leaders in their own right!

This allows me to delegate even more from my plate. They win by becoming better leaders, and I am free to lead from freedom!

I'm a huge proponent of innovations that will help grow the company. I love hearing great ideas from my team members. Because they know as the company makes a greater impact and increases our income, they also reap the benefits. So, when I look for a new team member, I'm always looking for innovative people. I want to know who is their client focus and who they're passionate about working with. I want to help them find innovative ways to work the schedule that is ideal for their chosen lifestyle and still meet client quotas.

We even work with them on their individual branding and messaging to attract their ideal clients. So they can be successful in their private practice within the structure of our agency. They really enjoy the flexibility and freedom of seeing themselves as successful in their own private practice.

We love our time outside of the practice! Times when we get together to socialize. I've set up a time for the team to get together to share life and business with each other without the "boss" listening in! They love this time together without me - so I'll keep supporting them in this community-building experiment!

Stepping into leadership began, for me, while working at a bank. The training that was provided helped me learn to be a good leader, and it was so important to choose a style of leadership that was heart-centered and aligned with me.

Working in customer service gave me the confidence to help cultivate other people's skills to shine and build their competence. I *knew* I was meant to be in supervisory and leadership positions! Even at the age of 20, I knew what the bank's needs were and proved to the manager that I had acquired the skills and mindset to be in management. I became an integral part of that bank's leadership team.

Eventually, my advocacy for others to grow led me to become a social worker. As other employees came to me with their problems, I knew I loved working with people within the leadership realm, which became invaluable in my private practice and starting my own practice.

That previous experience in leadership at the bank gave me the foundation that I needed since there was no leadership training offered in my master's program for social work. No one offered to help another cultivate those skills of leadership. I've seen what I don't want, so it became very clear to me what I did want.

Burnout among clinicians is real. You don't have the flexibility and autonomy that would be supportive when working for other agencies. I knew that would be integral in my marketing as I was searching for my team at my agency. I wanted to offer the kind of leadership that I knew they longed for.

As a team, we collaborate on so many levels. We support one another. We refer clients to one another when another team member's expertise would help. We have a very holistic approach to a multi-specialty private agency. We also cultivate marketing for each team member founded around their skills to attract their ideal clients. Knowing what their professional goals are, enhances their own growth within our agency.

I believe in an abundant mindset and cultivate that in all of my team members! We are a community of collaborators, so when we support each other, we all rise and make a greater impact on the world - at the same time, increasing our income!

We collaborate as we offer workshops on wellness. And, there's not just one model for all. Each therapist is allowed to choose what they are most passionate about and serve from their joy. We love it when we are all in our genius zone and celebrating each other's strengths. We have the freedom to move within the collaboration, but we're still a cohesive unit.

When offering group programs or workshops are not the passion of some of our therapists, we have the flexibility to honor each therapist's professional goals and offer the services they are passionate about. If they are not ready to diversify their income in that way, and they are meeting their client quotas, we want to support them in finding other creative ways to make a greater impact and increase their income.

Owning this agency has certainly offered me the opportunity for growth. I feel that my need for perfectionism and the feeling of being *not-enough* as a leader is something I'm having to unlearn and grow through. I'm always asking the question, *This is wonderful, but what else can I do for you?* I've had to realize that they are satisfied and I've done enough, so that takes the pressure off me. I'm learning to trust myself and the vision I'm holding. I'm learning to trust that it really is working out!

I know it didn't start out that way because I had so much fear around not being enough or even getting triggered by my attachment wounds and feeling abandoned. I just *knew* I wasn't doing enough, and people would leave my staff. But, I had to learn to be okay when people left. If we were not aligned anymore, I needed to make peace with them leaving.

As women leaders, many of us have not cultivated that competence or learned to feel secure in our confidence. We must hold the vision that we are making decisions for the best and highest good. Then, others will be able to catch our vision. We must know our *why* - as visionaries, our *why* is so important.

I hold the vision for what my practice stands for and the *why* of our mission. That is the overall structure of why we do the work we're doing. But, we also allow the feminine energy to flow together. We work together with no competition. Our leadership system seems to feel more like family - it feels more authentic.

When we experience struggles in our business, I can be transparent with my team. When a therapist struggles, we can openly address their issues in a non-threatening or demeaning way. We carry each others' burdens, and it eases the load for each of us. We are all rooting for each other!

All of our therapists are invested in this business. They are involved, and they are more inclined to want to help grow the business. We rise together!

This style of leadership is so much more fulfilling, personally. Not only are we making an impact on our community of clients, but we are also growing and making an impact on the lives of our staff. I am a huge proponent of self-care, not only for myself but also for my team members. Even this gives me a sense of fulfillment.

When I've gone through pivots in my business as I need to gain more skills to serve as the company's leader. Many of these skills have been learned on my own because there is no training during our schooling. As I've learned to perform payroll and other technical skills, it feels so exciting because I never fathomed that I would be able to talk about numbers, and they are meaningful! As a leader, I've built a lot of confidence. It just feels good. Even on the days, I want to run away, I go back to my *why* of wanting to create an impact.

Honing my business skills by helping my therapists develop their branding and marketing, accounting, and understanding reports has eased them into making a greater impact. Writing my therapists' biographies has helped them see themselves as worthy and dynamic experts for their client's benefit. It's always a journey of transformation for our clients and us. Our question is always, *What can we learn that will, in the end, benefit the clients?*

My goal for transformation for myself, my therapists, and our clients is to decide what's best from my gut. It may not align with business gurus, but I know it's right for me. I love hiring therapists and cultivating their new skills and honing their mastery, and especially their confidence as they transform and grow. So, we work together to understand what their professional goals are and work toward the skills that will get them there. I want to help them trust their own clinical skills. It can cause them some fear of learning how to confront clients during their therapy because their clients may want to leave. Done with gentleness, the clients are the winners with their own transformation.

It takes time, energy, and money to focus on leadership that cultivates their skills. As they gain confidence and trust in their clinical skills, they venture into new areas of therapy. Sometimes, they even enjoy the new area of treatment and find it so rewarding they pivot their focus!

When my therapists think they can't work with a specific clientele or issue, I allow them to test it out. They are scheduled for a few sessions in this new area and grow in confidence as they learn new skills or techniques. This is so exciting!

I want my therapists to experience the best professional life that fits into their desired lifestyle. I want to understand how much rest is needed, when they need a vacation, and how much time they need with their family. As long as they are happy and still fulfilling their client quota, I want them to be autonomous with a well-balanced life. This alleviates burnout.

Our clients receive great transformation. We know this because each quarter, we have an assessment of their treatment plan and what they are experiencing. Many of our clients have PTSD, significant childhood trauma, and mental disorders, yet have found relief and changed lives because of our services. Receiving these reports is so fulfilling.

As my practice is growing, I am expanding my team not only with therapists but also with administrative staff. If we always come from a place of curiosity, we can support each other and get what each of us needs. When we develop a space of safety, we can all grow through curiosity rather than demanding perfection.

I'm their biggest cheerleader! I affirm them and give feedback. As we talk through any of their struggles or learning curves, we can always come up with the next steps. They get excited for themselves.

In my style of leadership, I am definitely empathetic and intuitive. I focus on my mission and values. Diversity and creating a safe space for people, especially people of color, to heal. I must feel the alignment when hiring a staff member because this is a community. The staff's camaraderie is an important aspect of our agency, so personal chemistry and compatibility help me choose the right people. We are passionate about our staff having a relationship even outside of work.

"When we develop a space of safety, we can all grow through curiosity rather than demanding perfection."

~Shawniel Chamanlal

About Shawniel Chamanlal, LCSW

Shawniel Chamanlal is a Licensed Clinical Social Worker, Keynote Speaker, and Founder of Healing Springs Wellness Center. Her team of diverse and culturally competent clinicians provides mental health therapy, nutritional counseling, relationship coaching, and a variety of groups and workshops to promote emotional wellness.

Shawniel's 15 years of clinical experience as a licensed therapist fuels her passion for empowering individuals to heal their trauma, resolve limiting beliefs, and achieve emotional wellness. She is a Fordham Graduate and has specialized training in EMDR (Eye Movement Desensitization and Reprocessing), Cognitive Behavioral Therapy, Reiki, and Mindfulness-Based Stress Reduction.

Connect with Shawniel:

www.HealingSpringsWellness.com

contact@shawniellcsw.com

www.instagram.com/healingspringswellness

www.ShawnielChamanlal.com

Notes

Chapter 10

Lead From the Center

Joan Reed Wilson

From my earliest memories, I have been a leader. As the first-born grandchild in a close-knit Italian family, being the leader of the pack of eight grandchildren (whose ages ranged from six months to ten years younger than mine) came naturally. I never analyzed my role; I just fell into it. In the work that I do now, assisting families with their estate plans and elder law planning, I have become fascinated with the roles people take on in their family structures.

As was in my case, first-born children are often leaders; it is natural and necessary. Even an age difference of only one or two years creates an enormous experience gap when you are only four or five years old. The younger children look up to the older ones, in awe of the vast life knowledge that those few extra years have provided. No matter how old the younger ones get, the older ones are always older and experience life's events first. The role often creates a sense of purpose and acceptance for the older children. It certainly did in my life.

As I got older, I sought out roles of leadership. I was on the executive board of my sorority in college. I served as the Editor-in-Chief of my law school journal. When I started my first job out of law school, I gravitated toward being the lead on cases, which got me into trouble as a first-year associate. The partners were supposed to serve in that role, and I was reprimanded for trying to rise above my station too quickly. Within a few years, I decided to step outside of the traditional law firm model and create my own law firm where I could use my leadership skills.

Which Came First: Leadership or Control?

But as a true solo with no employees, was this leadership? Looking back twenty years later, I realize it was not. What I was seeking was autonomy and control. In the traditional, hierarchical structure of a business, leaders have the ultimate decision-making authority and, therefore, have a sense of control. I wanted this level of control in my law practice. I wanted to be able to decide which types of law I would practice, when I would work, which cases I would take, and how to manage the cases. Hanging my own shingle gave me this, but it was not until my firm started to grow and I hired my first employee that my leadership skills developed.

In my experience, leadership and control often go hand-in-hand. Leaders have more control over the organizations they lead than others in those organizations. But when control becomes the driving force, true leadership is quashed. Micromanagement is a well-known, negative term that defines a leader who controls too much. Yet the ultimate success or failure of an organization is usually accredited to the leader. So while micromanagement on one side of the continuum is not the best way to run a business or family, a leader does have to ensure the quality of work. It is a balancing act and one that I believe all leaders must continually navigate.

Unpacking Control

At the time I began my firm and started hiring employees, I was also a new mom, navigating the world of how to raise children. Having children is probably the best way for someone who likes control to bust through their old ways and learn to live, work, and manage without full control. Babies and toddlers do not care that you have been a leader all your life or that you have certain expectations for the day. My stages of losing control probably resembled some of the stages of grief.

At first, I was in denial and tried to push through with what I had intended to accomplish. Then I became angry that I could not get to what I wanted to. Finally, I began to bargain with my baby or with myself. "If I'm able to get her a really good feeding, get her burped and changed, then I will still have time to get to the grocery store and the post office, but if it takes a long time to burp her, then I'll just go to the grocery store."

It was not until I could accept the loss of control that I could also fully immerse myself in the wonder of the interactions with my daughter. Even though I was older and had more life experience and, as the parent, was meant to be the teacher and caregiver, I learned so much from her. Had I continued to push and bargain for my need to control the outcomes to meet my expectations, I would not have allowed myself to be open to accepting what the time with my daughter provided to me and our relationship.

The Flood Gates Open

Once I finally allowed myself to push through the need to control outcomes, I could focus on the benefit of the results. It also allowed me to reflect on situations in my past where I confused my need to control with leadership. There was the time I was Editor-in-Chief of the law journal, and we had a group meeting to discuss some concerns. One junior member of the journal raised her hand and brought up something that immediately made my entire body tense up. She basically called out something that made me feel like a bad leader. It triggered me before I knew anything about triggers. I immediately shut her down. It was definitely not one of my proudest moments and something that has stuck with me for over 25 years.

As I analyzed my reaction with the benefit of over two decades of hindsight, I was able to peel away the layers to the root of what caused my reaction. It was deeper than wanting to have control; it was fear of being wrong because someone who was born into a leadership role, whose existence is intertwined with being the person who others look up to, and whose self-worth revolves around having the answers equates to being wrong to being unlovable.

Luckily, this self-reflection occurred as I was building my business, hiring employees, and partnering with other lawyers. It took time to finally get to the realization that I do not need to have all of the answers to be lovable and successful. This quote from Mary Barra, the CEO of General Motors, is something I use to remind myself when that underlying feeling rears its ugly head: "It's okay to admit what you don't know. It's okay to ask for help. And it's more than okay to listen to the people you lead – in fact, it's essential."

Beginning to Strike a Balance

With this newfound enlightenment, as I continued to build my business with a partner and three employees, I was able to let go of the need to control every aspect of my business. The realization that I do not always have to be right and the knowledge that everyone has something unique and valuable to bring to the table opened up my world. I was able to rely on others, which I understand now was a necessary step to becoming a successful leader. If you do not let yourself rely on others, then you are not leading them; you are controlling them.

Of course, in any business, the end result still matters for success. Once you allow yourself to rely on others, it is still important to ensure that your product is valued and valuable. The quality of what your business produces needs to live up to your standards and the standards of your clientele. Good leadership is delegating tasks while ensuring quality results.

"If you do not let yourself rely on others, then you are not leading them; you are controlling them."

~Joan Reed Wilson

About Joan Reed Wilson

Joan Reed Wilson is the Managing Partner and founder of RWC, LLC, Attorneys and Counselors at Law, located in Middletown, Connecticut. Reed Wilson Case (RWC) is an all-female law firm. The RWC team assists clients in the areas of estate planning, elder law, Medicaid planning, conservatorships, probate and trust administration, and real estate closings.

Attorney Wilson is the President-elect of the CT Chapter of the National Academy of Elder Law Attorneys (NAELA), member of the Elder Law Section of the Connecticut Bar Association, accredited with the PLAN of CT for Pooled Trusts and with the Veteran's Administration. In 2021, Joan was appointed to the Governor's Task Force to Study Ways to Protect Senior Citizens from Fraud. And from 2017-2020, Attorney Wilson was one of 15 attorneys chosen by the Connecticut Attorneys Title Insurance Company (CATIC) to serve on its advisory committee.

While not at work, Joan is a wife, mother, friend, and active community member. Raised in Guilford, Joan received her Bachelor of Arts degree in Economics from Lehigh University in 1992 and her law degree from Boston University School of Law, cum laude, in 1997, where she served as Editor-in-Chief of the American Journal of Law & Medicine. She lives in Wethersfield with her husband, Jim Case, and her family.

Connect with Joan:

(860) 669-1222

jwilson@reedwilsoncase.com

www.facebooks.com/joanreedwilson

www.linkedin.com/in/joanreedwilson

Notes

Chapter 11
Growing a Heart-Led Team

Elizabeth B. Hill, MSW

I have felt the call to leadership since I was a child.

It started with me ordering my poor, sweet flowerchild of a mother around. Whether it was playing "school" where I was the teacher and she the student, an elaborate reenactment of a Magnum PI episode, or a long and tedious tour of the science museum I had set up in our basement, my dear mother was game. I am so grateful she went along with my creative whims.

School was the same. I had a wide variety of clubs. I started the Tangi club in second or third grade. Tangi club consisted of me bringing Tangi, a marionette, to school, and making people watch me play with the marionette.

Tangi was an orange bird on strings. She had a long torso made up of styrofoam spheres painted orange. She had big, bright eyes with beautiful, long black lashes. She had a bright orange feather that stuck out of her head. I hadn't made this Tangi bird, nor do I remember where she came from. Her strings were constantly getting tangled, but we persisted. I'd like to think I shared and let others take turns playing with Tangi. I'd like to believe I was that person. But I don't know that I was. A club in which I just made people watch me is pretty lame, but, unfortunately, in the world of clubs, this is a thing that can happen.

Grasshopper Club began in fourth grade. We would find grasshoppers during recess and put them in little bug houses. We did not do anything about feeding them because they just eat grass, right? Did we even give them water? I don't know. But I don't remember any of them dying. On Fridays, we would have Grasshopper Races. We would line them up and race them. One particularly tragic moment was when a friend's grasshopper won the race, and in her glory, she jumped around and then crushed the grasshopper under her foot. A tragic death. At least he died at the height of his glory.

The most uncomfortable and awkward club was the Kinky Club. I didn't know what the word kinky meant. My mother had permed her long, brown hair, and dad said it was kinky and laughed and laughed. I liked her hair, and I liked laughter, so it seemed a fun word. I don't know what the Kinky Club was supposed to be about. But I made a shirt that said Kinky Club on it with these crayon/marker thingies you could make t-shirts from.

My mother, sadly, let me leave the house in this shirt. A wise and kind (thank God) boy in my class came over and said to me, "do you know what kinky means?" I don't remember exactly what he said or how he got me clued in, but he let me know it was sexual in nature. I don't remember being too horrified about it, but I did have the sense to not ever wear the shirt again.

I think there was also a club about horses because my friends and I used to spend a lot of time running around like horses during recess. (And if I spent time on something, I had probably given it an organizational name.) From the people that got to ride real horses, I learned the terms gallop, trot, and canter, and that male stallions can be evil jerks to young geldings. We would act out these dramas in the field by the elementary school, running free as horses, neighing and whinnying. One of our friends became a veterinarian, so it seems like all this play-acting worked out well for her professionally. I went on to act silly and ridiculous, so I guess it worked out for me too.

In college, I was Treasurer of Theatre Unlimited, then President. I formed CCSU4Peace with two of my friends in the wake of the 9-11 attacks. In grad school, I did my best to re-awaken the Progressive Students Alliance and helped organize students to attend peace rallies and protests in Washington, D.C. and Hartford, Connecticut.

During grad school and after, I worked for nonprofits. I was often put in charge of things that were way over my head. In my early 20s, I was put in charge of leading a monthly meeting of strategic planners, a very important role at the nonprofits. Many of them had been in the work for decades. It never felt like I was given roles because people saw an ability in me. It felt like no one else wanted to do it - and I didn't know how to say no.

In the nonprofit world, I got good at doing things that no one else wanted to do - compiling data reports, calculating return-on-investment (ROI) for social programs, and writing up client success stories. I once had to speak in front of a group as a keynote speaker - woefully unprepared and totally bombed. It. Was. Horrible. But I survived.

I now have the great blessing to have chosen to step into leading a company that helps people get their dream of a book (such as this one) into print. In some ways, this also was thrust upon me. I did not set out to be a writing coach or publisher, but the universe left me breadcrumbs, and I followed.

I would learn one thing about writing or publishing, and then someone would come to me with a new challenge. My answer was never, "sorry, I don't know how, you'll have to find someone else."

It was always... "so I've not done that before, but I'm sure I can find someone who has."

One by one, I gathered people around me that knew more than me about particular things. I learned from them and they learned from me. Because of this collaborating, I now have a team of amazing people that work for or are collaborating with Green Heart Living Press. All of us know more than each other about something. We have a shared reverence for one another.

I'm honest about what I know and don't know. I am eager to have people's feedback and learn from them. I admit when I've made a mistake. I ask for forgiveness when I mess up.

I've been transparent with them about business growth. I don't pretty it up. I share when we've had lower revenue months than expected. I have shared when we've hit over $10K/month. As of this writing, we just hit our first ever over $20K month. We never would have scaled to this if I followed my old model of running the show on my own.

While we are a collaborative team, I do know that as the owner of the company, there are some things I take ultimate responsibility for. If a client is unhappy, I have the responsibility to make it right. I have to file taxes. I need to know all the parts of the business so I can jump in as needed. I need to look at the big picture and make sure each task has at least two people on the team that can do the task.

I check in with my team to make sure they are doing things that align with their life goals. I want to give them assignments that they find fulfilling, and that will help them grow towards their ultimate goals.

Right now, the team includes an online business manager, writing coaches, a book marketing and launch expert, editors/formatters, a brand photographer/ videographer, and a brand designer who has taken our book covers and launches to the next level. Some of our team members wear multiple hats. I've recently brought on a CPA to do bookkeeping, my taxes, and help with some financial strategy for growing profits. I also have an attorney that is helping guide trademarks. I've hired people to help build courses. Some of these I've paid directly. Some I've built packages that include them so that they get paid as we sell packages. Some are being paid through structured education and assistance in building their businesses. Since the business is my only household income, it had to grow in a way that met my family income needs while paying my team at a level where they felt respected and honored for their work.

Behind all of this are coaches. For me and the business. Since I trained as a life coach six years ago, I've learned that having a coach expands the quality of my life and eases my burden so much that I have no desire to do life without a coach anymore. So whenever I have a project that feels like a huge weight or that I feel overwhelmed by, I get a coach for it. We collaborate together on whatever projects in my life I need help with.

My life coach Kathleen Troy has been my constant support for years, holding space for me as I grow, heal, and make a better life for my kids and me while building my business. Along the way, I've hired business coaches, an organizational coach, and a wellness coach. I'm a pretty amazing lady. I own this. AND, my coaches have helped me achieve things and experience life in ways that I would never have gotten to on my own.

When I tried to build my life coaching business on my own, it did work. I'm not saying it didn't. I had clients and they got results. I made money, but it wasn't enough money to support my kids and me. I was still having to work other jobs in the nonprofit field that, while allowing for a lot of flexibility for my family, were still very high stress with a small paycheck.

When I opened up to the coordinating expertise of the universe (aka allowing other people to collaborate with me) everything shifted.

If collaboration makes you feel afraid, there's probably a good reason for it! I'd recommend reading Dr. Davia Shepherd's book "Grow Smarter," where she talks about what makes a good collaboration. If you are afraid of collaborating, it's probably because you were in collaboratives where you got hurt, taken advantage of, or where you had to do too much (or all!) of the work. There's a whole other way of experiencing collaboration. I'm grateful for Dr. Davia and all my dear Ladies' Power Lunch and Green-Hearted clients and team members who have shown me another way to grow.

Here are my recommendations when growing a team for your soul-aligned business:

- Always look for the win-win-win (a win for me, the team member, and your clients).

- Be honest and transparent; share your wins and your losses.

- Use a healthy balance of masculine and feminine energy in your collaborative work.

- Be intentional in learning about people's big dreams and create opportunities for them to grow toward them.

- Be clear on your values and those of your company, and cultivate a team that reflects that.

- Learn to receive.

- Learn more about yourself and your human design (or whatever personality type guidance clicks with you) and build a business that utilizes those qualities.

Now Green Heart Living feels like a giant club. My Green Heart Team now feels like a club with the kinship of a family. So I put all my good experience of organizing people around orange marionettes, grasshoppers, and words that I did not know the meaning of, to good use. (Now I keep a dictionary nearby, always.)

If you are looking for a way to expand your leadership and grow your business in a new collaborative way, think of what lit you up as a child. If you tap into that, you may just find the spark you need to grow your business in a soul-aligned way.

"When I opened up to the coordinating expertise of the universe (aka allowing other people to collaborate with me) everything shifted."

~ Elizabeth B. Hill

About Elizabeth B. Hill, MSW

Elizabeth B. Hill, MSW, is the CEO and founder of Green Heart Living and Green Heart Living Press. She is the author of *Be the Beacon, Embrace Your Space, Success in Any Season, The Great Pause: Blessings and Wisdom from COVID-19, Love Notes: Daily Wisdom for the Soul,* and *Green Your Heart, Green Your World: Avoid Burnout, Save the World and Love Your Life.*

Elizabeth coaches clients on mindful leadership and writing to heal, inspire, and grow their impact in the world. Trained as a social worker, yoga teacher, and ontological coach, she weaves creativity, spirituality, and mindfulness into her work with clients. With over 15 years of experience writing and leading collaborations in the nonprofit sphere, Elizabeth brings a uniquely engaging approach to collaborative book projects. Elizabeth lives in a historic (and hysterical) home in Connecticut with her children, Raven and James.

Connect with Elizabeth:

www.GreenHeartLiving.com

Notes

Part Four

Leading with Your Own Light

Chapter 12

Shying Away from the Spotlight

Teresa Hnat

Jack Jacker Elementary school. 1990.

A shy girl with blond hair and boxy bangs sits in her first-grade classroom. She's trying to write in her workbook, but she's having trouble doing so. Her pencil has been worn down so far that the wood sticks out further than the graphite. She eyes the sharpener across the room where it sits by the window. The pencil desperately needs to be sharpened, but the girl doesn't move. Instead, she worries. She worries that the simple act of getting up will draw attention. What if she trips? What if the teacher yells at her? What if she can't figure out how to use the sharpener, and she looks like an idiot, and the other kids laugh? Nope, it's much safer to stay seated and try to make this pencil work as long as possible.

Meet 8-year-old Teresa. Painfully shy, quiet, anxious, and doing whatever she could do to stay out of the spotlight. Even if it meant wearing down pencils so far, they were unusable. But 8-year-old Teresa is also creative, observant, empathetic, and a great listener. She doesn't realize how much these qualities will help her thrive and be a leader later in life.

My whole life, I have been quiet, thoughtful, and shy. I've been told to "smile more" or "be more outgoing." The qualities of shyness, quietness, and empathy were viewed as weaknesses.

For so long, I believed this was true. For the better part of my teens and early twenties, I wished for the ability to be big and bold.

My opportunity came in an unexpected place, a portrait studio. During my mid-twenties, I got my first real job working for a photographer. Her studio was like nothing I'd ever seen before. Two floors housed a total of four different studios plus three changing rooms, a lounge, a sales room, a large waiting area, and an onsite print lab, which was where I was going to be working.

Along with the owner, there were two other photographers, a graphic designer, a sales associate, and various part-time assistants. The portraits they created were like nothing I had seen before. The walls were lined with 24 x 30 canvas prints that showcased portraits that were not simple snapshots but creative works of art. Instantly I was hooked.

The studio quickly became more than just a job, but working there was intimidating. My experience was in the print lab. Everything else was foreign to me. The ladies I worked with were gorgeous, put together, and so self-assured. I, on the other hand, was currently riding the hot mess express. I was limping along on a crutch, still healing from a knee injury. I wore shapeless, oversized clothing, trying to hide my weight gain. How would I ever fit in with these radiant, confident Goddesses?

Instead, I did what I did best, I quietly watched and observed from the sidelines, soaking in everything I could. I watched where they put lights, how they talked to clients and how they directed them, how they got them to smile naturally and how they put them at ease. I had never realized how much photographers needed to take charge and lead!

When people step in front of the camera, they feel like the spotlight is on them, but in reality, at that moment, the spotlight is on the photographer. A good photographer doesn't stand quietly snapping photos and waiting for their client to pose themselves. A good photographer leads! They confidently guide that client through every pose, every smile, and every moment of that shoot.

It would mean talking to clients non-stop to put them at ease. (*But what if I couldn't think of anything to say?*) It meant being a comedian, cracking jokes to make their client smile. (*Jokes?! But I'm not funny!*) It was guiding clients through poses, showing them how to tilt their heads, place their hands, and everything in between. (*What if I can't think of any poses? What if my mind goes blank?*)

The thought of taking charge like this was daunting and intimidating. There was just no way a goofy, awkward, shy gal like me could confidently lead and direct a stranger.

As the years went by, my role at the studio expanded. I had added to my arsenal of skills, not just a trained eye but graphic design and retouching, and I had become proficient with a camera.

It was around this time that the inquiries began to come in.

Can you photograph my wedding?

My family?

My baby?

Each time friends or family asked, I said no until one day, my brother asked if I could do engagement photos for him. This time there was no backing out, no excuse I could give. He was my brother! Besides, he wasn't a stranger; maybe it wouldn't be too scary....

Nope! I was wrong! From the moment I arrived, they looked to me for instruction and guidance, little of which I could provide. I tripped over my words about as much as I tripped over my own feet. I stuttered and stammered, and I was so focused on trying to get everything to come together I was stone serious. This was clearly not for me because I was shy, introverted, and quiet.

The years continued to roll by. I watched as the studio owner continued to learn new techniques and styles. I watched as her work won awards, and I fell even more in love with the art of photography.

There was a portrait that hung outside the lab. I'd walk by it a dozen times every day, and often, I would pause to look at it. It depicted a young woman in a bright orange leotard with a long tulle skirt and gold ballet pointe shoes. One of her legs was extended with her toe pointed out in front of her and was slightly submerged in a pool of ripply water, casting her reflection back up at her.

Ever since I had seen this specific portrait, I had been entranced. And for the first time ever on my journey, I felt wistful. I wanted to create portraits like this! Portraits that were bold, creative works of art.

After years of doing nothing more than photographing flowers, landscapes, and animals, I had grown bored. It's in my nature to look for a challenge, especially a creative one, and people were to be my next creative challenge. With much apprehension, I started to work on my portfolio.

For over a year, every single session was an anxiety-filled nightmare!

Every.

Single.

Session.

I would spend every drive fretting over what I would do, my heart racing with fear. I'd think, *"Am I always going to feel this way? Will it ever feel different?"*

Every session went in a similar fashion. I'd stumble my way

through directing clients. *"Um, yeah, um, maybe, um, put your hand um, there on your waist."*

I'd frantically be searching my notes on my phone for pose ideas while they were changing. Guzzling water because my anxiety was so bad I was getting dry mouth.

Yup, that was me. Red-faced, sweaty, and stuttering, I was hardly the picture of a confident photographer.

Every drive home, I felt dazed and exhausted. I was convinced that this is how I would always feel. It would always be scary.

But, for some reason, I kept doing it. I am stubborn, and I don't like to admit failure. And deep down, there was a part of me that loved photographing people. It was challenging! It was thrilling! People are dimensional, they're inspiring, fascinating, and they are certainly complex! It's one thing to snap a photo, but it's a whole other skill set to be able to capture a story and the essence of a person in a single photograph. It was this complexity that kept things fresh and exciting.

I narrowed my focus to brand photography, working with women who were small business owners. I also started looking inward, at my own feelings, specifically around anxiety. I knew most people have anxiety when it comes to stepping in front of the camera. But why? Where did their anxiety stem from? And where did mine stem from?

I had conversations. I asked friends, family, past clients, current clients, and my networking groups why they were anxious about stepping in front of the camera. While there was a lot of expected anxiety around "looking good," a big proponent of anxiety was simply not knowing what to do. They felt unprepared. They didn't know what to wear or how to pose themselves.

Many of the women I spoke with also talked about having

negative experiences getting their photos taken in the past. They felt that the photographer they worked with didn't listen to them or didn't take the time to truly understand who they were and what they were looking for.

I started to realize that some of the most important work took place before the photoshoot ever began. It was the conversations I would have with clients during their sales call and planning calls. I started asking even more questions, deeper questions, and listening more. As my clients would speak to me, their words would become visual images in my head, which I would furiously write down.

The added bonus of having such deep conversations ahead of their session is on shoot day; we didn't feel like two strangers meeting for the first time.

I also started giving even more directions to my clients. I never expected anyone to know how to pose, but I realized that perhaps I wasn't giving enough support and communication in this area. I started showing clients exactly how I wanted them to pose or what I wanted them to do. I constantly talked to them, encouraged them, and asked them how they were feeling throughout the process. It's important to me that what we're doing and creating together feels true to them and not staged or faked.

I let go of the notion that I needed to come into every session full of loud, boisterous energy. That just wasn't me, and it was exhausting trying to pretend it was. Instead, I would come into sessions as just me - quiet, calm, and a little quirky. As soon as I started embracing these qualities, a funny thing happened, clients started commenting on how calming my presence was during a session. They'd tell me they had started the day feeling nervous but as soon as we began their session, they felt calm and completely comfortable.

Once I embraced my own qualities, another amazing thing happened- my imagery got better and better. This was because I wasn't focused on myself anymore. Thoughts like, *"do I look stupid doing this?"* and *"am I being funny enough?"* were gone. Instead, I started to hyper-focus on my clients, opening myself up to inspiration and finding the best ways to visually portray their story and their true essence.

The best part of being a photographer is helping open someone's eyes to their own star quality. Most of my clients are shy, introverted, and not completely confident in the spotlight. But when I capture them, I mean truly capture their spirit, and they finally see themselves the way the rest of us see them, it can be life-changing. They finally see their beauty, their heart, and their gifts! Being able to witness someone finally embrace their true qualities, confidently step into their spotlight, and embrace being the star of their business, is beyond rewarding.

I feel like a proud mama watching them shine so brightly. Several have gone on to not only create six-figure businesses, but they have now become leaders in their industries!

I often pause and marvel at all these amazing people who have come into my life. How did this shy, quiet girl, who was afraid to sharpen her pencil, manage to surround herself with so many talented, heart-centered, inspirational leaders?

As soon as I started to embrace my own qualities as strengths instead of weaknesses, everything began to change. And then one day....it happened. I was driving to a session and....I was excited! My brain was buzzing with all the things I wanted to do, all the poses I wanted to use. And the anxiety... was just a dull hum in the background. Whoa. These days I'm still red-faced, sweaty, and guzzling water, but only because I'm always running around full of inspiration and excitement.

We are taught that leaders are born, not made. Those of us

who are shy, quiet, introverted, or have anxiety are not cut out for leading. It's the brave, the bold, and the charismatic that are meant to be leaders. But I want to challenge that notion. I think those of us who are quiet, anxious, or introverted can and should lead. The qualities of shyness, empathy, and sensitivity, shouldn't be looked at as weaknesses. They are, in fact, some of the best strengths a person can have. The best leaders are those who listen and those who understand others. Those who don't seek the spotlight are often better suited for it.

"I think those of us who are quiet or anxious or introverted can and should lead. The qualities of shyness, empathy, and sensitivity, shouldn't be looked at as weaknesses. They are, in fact, some of the best strengths a person can have."

~Teresa Hnat

About Teresa Hnat

Teresa Hnat is a professional photographer and videographer helping therapists and heart-led entrepreneurs build an impactful visual brand so they can scale their practices.

During a session, it's likely you'll see her rearrange furniture, lay on the ground, and get really excited about lighting. She wants each session to be an experience. After all, having photos taken shouldn't be a hassle, it should be fun! It's a celebration of everything that has been accomplished!

Teresa is a member of the PPA (Professional Photographers of America). She believes in the importance of staying up to date in the knowledge of photography and videography.

Connect with Teresa:

www.TeresaHnat.com

Notes

Chapter 13
The Power of the Collective

Kathleen Troy

Oh, the irony! While shopping at Lowe's, I noticed a new T-shirt stand with logos affixed. One stood out to me: "If you want something done right, do it yourself!" As I have been thinking so much about collaboration and what had me go from being undercover anonymous, doing it all myself, to preferring group collaboration, I think I've traced it. This archaic T-shirt motto encompasses so much of my early, uninformed state of mind.

I think I have traced the basis of what makes people think it is preferable to do things alone than to count on others or look for support. When I forage through the memories of my youth, I observe a very studious, quiet, purposeful student from a very young age. I wanted to do well. We're going back to the late 60s and early 70s. (I was born in 1964 in blue-collar Michigan. It was a very different mentality back then.)

The teaching model, from my current perspective, was to excel at independent study. Competition had not yet been questioned. Spelling Bees were cutthroat, and we rarely paired up or "grouped" up for projects. We were not given writing prompts and had to squirm with discomfort until we had any inspiration. Copying was met with wrath from fellow students. It was not considered a compliment! I learned through this that I was blessed with creative thoughts and fiercely guarded them. It was all I knew!

I loved *not* collaborating. I was shy and creative. I thrived on independent thought processes; it was my comfort zone. Upon occasion, we were ordered to complete group reports. When I was in a pair or foursome, I would have to talk, and this was very challenging for me because I was intensely self-conscious. I would end up shouldering the work for the group because I was driven, and I could get it done. Often, the other kids wouldn't do their part, and I'd end up doing more than my share. I took it all so seriously. It did not occur to me to take a stand and call upon the others to rise to the occasion. I had no capacity to confront others and was desperate to be liked more than to be respected. We did not yet know the word "anxiety" to describe this level of discomfort.

I saw the difference between when my daughters were in school versus when I was immersed in my studies. Some of the things that shifted were that my daughters' New York schools were very intentional about having children work collaboratively. Society had shifted, and so did education. When they had to do oral reports, sharing the limelight, the group would have a different segment of the report. They produced book reports solo, but the projects were definitely collaborative.

One aspect of collaboration in the classroom never seems to change. I observed that teachers would often pair my daughters with students who were easily distracted or confused. My older daughter, Jameyla, was more studious and quiet like me. Inevitably, she would be paired with students who were not serious, and I could feel her frustration increase as she, too, was left to shoulder the burden: tying up the loose ends and finishing other students' segments so that it would be done on time.

Sofia was not as diligent, and there may have been a student or two carrying her responsibilities over the finish line. Yet, she was often artfully placed near easily distracted students or those who struggled to follow directions and was at times frustrated as well by class antics. She found it easier to isolate than to work with the person sitting beside her.

For people like me, or my daughters, doing it alone just became easier than depending on others and having them - the collective - fail. I recognize the familial pattern of not learning to speak up for ourselves. I still had not developed strategies for confrontation and passed this weakness down the line. I hear this lament in discussions with women in the workforce. Scratch the surface, and the stories of mismatched teams at work come spilling forth. And the stakes are higher. If you are not a "team player," no matter how mismatched, it could affect your livelihood.

I now realize that it takes confidence to collaborate. When we choose our collaborators and are not involved through default or randomly assigned partners, a remarkable sensation occurs.

The energetic undercurrent of feeling confident enough to brainstorm with others and consider new ideas not yet formed by each individual is best described as a "cosmic elixir." I now find that I've collaborated with people whose genius zones complement mine.

There is a zone where you wake up with an idea that pops in overnight. Have you enjoyed this phenomenon? I see it in my husband often. He will puzzle over a broken tool or mysterious engine noise. It will be the last thing he dissects before lights out. Inevitably, he wakes up with the answer. It is pure joy!

I do that, too. I'll ask for clarity. Upon waking, I see the blockage from a whole different light. It is magical! And how stimulating it is to share the sparks of inspiration with other people who are receptive! To experience the confidence and trust to share this new idea: this is the next-level child's play!

Four years ago, I was invited to facilitate a workshop for women staff members at the United Nations. Sara, a new member of my networking group, approached me after hearing me share my coaching "elevator pitch." She stated, "I hear you speak about focusing on men but do you like to speak with women too? Do you like to?"

"Absolutely! I just find that most coaches choose women. It appeared that men trust me, and I am curious about them, so as a coach, I remain curious. Yet, I love supporting women, and I've done a lot of work with them."

(You see, as a hair colorist for over 30 years, women inspired me to be a coach because they often remarked that I gave them perspective or I believed in them when few others did.)

"I'd love for you to do a workshop for the women staffers at the UN."

Sara coordinated programs for monthly Lunch Bunch Friday workshops there. I was so excited. That would definitely be a dream come true. I knew the topic I most wished to share: Healthy Priorities as an interactive tool.

I shared this exchange with another fairly new friend, Stacy. She immediately said, "Let me support you! You'll need support. You'll need somebody to take a photo of you. You will need someone to help you set up and to keep you calm that day. I can be your assistant!"

This had not even occurred to me. I never thought to ask for support, even as a coach who encourages clients to ask for support! When Stacy offered, I was incredulous. "You really would like to go? With me?" At that moment, I felt so special.

I can't even begin to describe how much more exciting that day was to have somebody in my corner who simply saw what I saw and understood that we weren't being paid in currency. The experience was the reward of a lifetime. Sharing the anticipation, and discussing after, was delightful. Stacy loves workshops as much as I do! She supported me in a way that allowed me to focus and enjoy myself. It is also a beautiful experience to have a witness to something that is so special to us.

The theme was healthy priorities and helping women to understand that they have to come first. They needed support. They were working in different time zones! For example, the Italian contingency had to be on the Italian clock and operate on Eastern Time. One Director came in a bit late and talked about how she had a baby who kept her up all night. Her three-year-old and workday schedule were on Eastern Time, but meetings were scheduled in Central European Time. Her sheer exhaustion showed.

The women bonded as they realized how much they had in common. They were paired with other women of different statuses and departments. Most had been too harried to notice the kindred spirits in their orbit. There is magic in speaking to a stranger, and they were able to experience the phenomenon. Women supporting other women is a remarkable gift.

My intention is to support people in remembering to be their own best friends and to open up to support. By doing so myself, I was able to see it for others.

Once you experience the art, joy, genius, and magic of collaboration, I tell you, it's like an elixir. You just want more. I almost don't even like to do things on my own now. I choose to experience the world from this vantage point. It is so very rich.

Our kinship through the Powerful Collective stands out as one of the richest collaborations I could wish for. And here is the irony: I saw a need and asked these women to join me initially for "holding space." They all saw the same need in their loved ones. As we progressed by organizing workshops, the synchronicity in our brainstorming was otherworldly. As we each developed our own program segment, it would mesh with the next and flow without much effort on our part. The synergy of this collective was palpable. Our participants felt it, too.

Collaboration is a gift I wish for every soul to experience!

"My intention is to support people in remembering to be their own best friend and to open up to support. By doing so myself, I was able to see it for others."

~Kathleen Troy

About Kathleen Troy

After many successful years in the NYC beauty industry and rearing two daughters with her husband of 34 years, Kathleen Troy became an ICF-certified Ontological Life Coach. She graduated in 2017 from a rigorous coach training program held in NYC, Accomplishment Coaching, and accessed her deeper purpose through this process.

Kathleen creates specialized sessions, tools, and exercises to meet her clients at their own emotional points of access. Whether it is a CEO, someone divorced, a single person, an empty nest parent, or a millennial, there is a journey of deep joy and purpose available, and Kathleen will partner with her clients to overcome circumstances, hurdles, and excuses as they create an intentional life.

Kathleen enjoys facilitating personal development workshops for small businesses, corporations, and collectives, yoga retreats in partnership with yoga specialists, and individual coaching sessions. She has facilitated a Women's Empowerment Session at the U.N. and was deeply moved by the powerful, vibrant women in attendance.

Connect with Kathleen:

www.SecondSpringCoaching.com

www.instagram.com/secondspringcoaching

www.linkedin.com/in/kathleentroy

Notes

Chapter 14

They Called it a Breakdown

Kelly McCarthy

The clinical world called it a breakdown, and for one heavily medicated year, I would have agreed with them had it not been for the voice inside me that began screaming as I took baby steps towards feeling something, anything, again.

It started out as a joke, really. My husband and I would take our son Brandon to karate class, and on the bulletin board in the lobby, there was a sign advertising a MissFits Bootcamp. Well, yeah, with my life as I perceived it at the time, I felt like one of those misfit toys in the classic movie Rudolph. I didn't know who to be, never really did; actually, I just knew I was no longer who I once was.

I looked the same, but most of the time, I was on autopilot. I didn't live life; I existed in it. I was better than I once was as the hopelessness was gone but numb to feeling much of anything more than what the medications would allow. My thoughts went from frantic to now echoing in a chamber with no answers because I didn't care, as I had no conscious understanding of what I was even missing. I was alive, and I thought that was good enough.

I realized years after taking that first step into the unknown as the newest member of MissFits Bootcamp that I was mistaken; there was so much more. I just hadn't learned, YET. The epiphany of the true meaning of MissFits came years later when I awakened to the power of my own perception. It now registers in my consciousness it was meant to say MISS FIT, which I had become emotionally, mentally, physically, and finally spiritually over time.

As I moved my body and was introduced to a nutritional system (yes, an MLM that will remain unnamed) I became stronger, and my need for the seven different medications I was on became less and less. Each month I was seen by a team of behavioral specialists attached to the hospital that would see me for all of five minutes, ask me the same questions every month and would sometimes listen and sometimes drag out their idea of what was best for me only to crush my dreams of removing all medications from my life. That's when the voice showed up loudly enough for me to take notice.

It was me, but the me I hadn't been introduced to yet. She was loud, strong, and not going away. She had been there listening, watching, waiting as I began to start believing in little parts of myself until finally, she said, "ENOUGH!" I stepped into her shadow for the very first time at the next scheduled visit with my team. They thought they knew what was best for me, but I stood my ground, asking to be readmitted to the hospital so I could safely start weaning off the medications. I refused to take no for an answer as they bullied me with their arguments, their misdiagnosis, and their titles. I simply said, "If you can't help me, I will find someone who will." I was back in the hospital the following week.

I will not say the rest of my journey into finding myself was easy. It was the exact opposite of easy at the time, but I was supported in a way I had never been before. The voice inside me, my own personal cheerleader, was getting stronger because the choices I was making were in alignment with who I was meant to be, and I didn't even know it yet. I had been a victim in my life for so long that I had no understanding of what it meant to take personal responsibility for my life and the path I was currently on.

It was far too easy to blame everyone and everything else for why I was exactly where I was.

I knew very little of the spiritual world, had never heard of the Law of Attraction, nor did I understand energetic frequencies and how much we imprint and impact every experience and every being on the planet, whether we are conscious of it or not. I seriously thought the MLM I was part of was brought into my life to lose weight, which I did and then gained it back; however, that's a whole other chapter in itself.

Instead, I have discovered it was meant to introduce me to some of the greatest thought leaders in the world which I had the privilege of working with, and these experiences, these people opened the door to learning about myself, about gratitude, victim mentality, forgiveness, mindset, LOA, healthy boundaries, meditation (something I kinda sorta dabbled in but not really and not with any intention) and so much more.

What I found truly remarkable as I look back on my experience with this company was that I had become a walking billboard for weight loss, and though it was the physical appearance that people noticed first, it was actually my energy, my ability to touch people's souls with my words as I stood in my truth even when it looked different from others that inspired others to begin their own journeys.

As I continued my journey into physical health as the "walking billboard" of looking good, I spent up to three hours a day pushing myself into something I thought I should be happy with. I went straight from the bootcamp style gym to running up to three miles a day (sometimes more), then off to a second gym for weight training or boxing with a personal trainer.

I became obsessed with what I looked like, what I fed my body (or didn't feed it), and received compliments and accolades from everyone everywhere, having released over 100 pounds and 100 inches in less than a year, which of course, fanned the fires to another frantic energy much like the restaurant business was that I had been a part since graduating high school. The attention was great, it supplied a sense of being something, but there was still a piece I was missing.

A lingering emptiness inside that would creep up on me, but no real understanding of what it was or why I was feeling it. I looked good, was eating right, was surrounded by positive affirmations, self-help books while hanging on to every word of any thought leader I was being introduced to through various avenues, and still, I wasn't truly happy.

It wasn't until one day I was in the gym hearing the voice of my various trainers in my head telling me, "You got this, Kels, just one more Kels, push it, Kels!!!" while doing 45 pound flyes, yes you read that right, and yes I had no business doing them, I literally felt and heard something in my left shoulder snap. I dropped the weights as the pain seared through my shoulder and literally got up, grabbed my post-workout shake bottle, and left in tears. That was the last day I ever stepped into a gym.

The revelation of not being able to go to the gym was absolutely devastating. It had become my whole world, my identity, and all I knew. I felt myself falling backward into a depressive state, when one morning, I awoke to an email from some company I had never heard of nor ever signed up to receive information on, but there it was, and the subject matter caught my eye, and I felt my heart skip a beat.

It said, "Heal Yourself Through the Power of Energy with Jeffrey Allen," or something to that effect. The cheerleader that lived inside my head perked up and instantly said "YES, click on it." and so I did. I found myself signing up for a live webinar with this guy I had never heard of and impatiently waiting for whatever he had to say. I remember feeling him before he even spoke, a feeling I had experienced before in my life but didn't have a word for.

He walked me and hundreds, maybe even thousands of others through this guided meditative energy session, and as I submitted to his energetic pull to relax and go within the excruciating pain I had been in and was told I would always have without surgery, completely disappeared in this one-hour session. I was hooked. I signed up for his ongoing training after the webinar, now a full believer in whatever this was as it had sparked a fire within my soul that I had never felt before. It was like coming home to a home I somehow remembered but had never experienced. It was my first glimpse of the universe literally having my back, as Gabby Bernstein would say, but seeing as I didn't know who she was yet, I didn't really know what that even meant.

As I think of all the times these serendipitous moments appeared in my unconscious life, the more I realize I was on the exact path I needed to be on to bring me to this moment right now. I know now the injury was a guided message from the universe that I wasn't living my purpose, not even close, and the only way I was going to listen was for them to literally pick me up and throw me down a different path, as they do from time to time, when I get stuck in my ego and refuse to listen. For that, I say with absolute gratitude, "Thank you, Universe."

As I deepened my practice and my understanding of energy work, I came to realize it was never the product of the MLM itself that I loved, it was the energy of the people around me that I was attracted to. The ability to see people exactly where they were and somehow trusting that I knew what to say in any given situation, and so I did and continue to do so.

The more I go within, the more I understand that every single one of us is doing the very best we can with what we perceive to know in that moment. And these perceptions are filtered through our own experiences, instilled beliefs, self-talk, and ego. Holding compassion for ourselves and those that see or think differently is key to understanding that no one is right or wrong in their own mind.

Instead of wasting time and energy trying to change anyone else, the biggest lesson I have learned on my personal journey is to be the best version of me in as many conscious moments of the day as possible with an open mind and an open heart. Maya Angelou once said, "As we know better, we do better, and as we do better, we help create space for others to do the same."

It was my calling to be the mirror for others, to help people remember the beautiful being they were born as before their conditioned life took over, leaving them on autopilot, unknowingly following the path of others instead of their own. Just by being me, I create conscious awareness for others around me. I openly share the importance of remembering the connection to self, others, Mother Earth, and the Animal Kingdom.

I surround myself with those that choose to live in a higher frequency and take personal responsibility for the energetic footprint they are leaving behind. We were never meant to live in the pain, suffering, and stories of our ancestor's ancestors, but instead, we are to consciously live in the opportunities, possibilities, and dreams of our children's children. To remember, as children, we lived in simplicity, stayed present in the moments, dreamt big, and believed even bigger.

I danced in the woods, in awe of my surroundings, and created magical potions from her bounty. I ran barefoot, connecting to her heartbeat, and the animals were my friends as I pretended to be them. And then, one day, I just stopped. Things out of my control took center stage as I was taught what was important and what wasn't. Stop daydreaming, focus, push, succeed, and win.

And before I knew it, I lost myself in a prison of thoughts, comparisons, beliefs, and ideas that weren't even mine. To come home to oneself is a practice that takes time to remember, patience, and self-compassion to learn, trust, and allow, but then one day, you wake up and realize it's no longer something you need to practice or do it's simply you who have become.

It's a choice to live with intention and conscious awareness, and it is what I choose. I live my life co-creating as one energy, dreaming my world into being with the understanding I am the ripple effect, and it's my choice each and every moment of each and every day of which ripple I will be. That I lead by energetic example through the power of my words and my actions.

It's not something I turn on when someone is watching or when a client walks through my door, it's who I am to the core of my being with the realization that I am a spiritual being having a human experience, and in this moment, I am doing the best I can with what I know.

I remember the day Michael Bernard Beckwith said to me, "Life is not happening to you, it's not even happening for you, it's happening as you, through you." That was the day I was catapulted into conscious awareness and realized the breakdown the clinical world labeled me with was, in fact, a breakthrough to learn to live a very different life than the one I thought I had to, and it was a conscious decision to release my ego and trust what I can't always see, but when I take the pause and go within, I always know.

"Instead of wasting time and energy trying to change anyone else, the biggest lesson I have learned on my personal journey is to be the best version of me in as many conscious moments of the day as possible with an open mind and an open heart."

~Kelly McCarthy

About Kelly McCarthy

Kelly McCarthy is an expert in understanding energetic frequencies and how we imprint and impact the world, whether consciously or unconsciously. As a former restaurant owner and mother of two, she was caught in the frantic energy of always trying to stay one step ahead, struggling to juggle both personal and professional life, with the need to slow down. After a hospital stay, which the clinical world would call a breakdown; Kelly saw it as a breakthrough to learn from a variety of modalities to help her remember her connection to her ancestors and the power of harnessing Universal Energy. As a spiritual leader in the holistic community, she was called to create her business, Beyond Words N Wisdom, sharing her knowledge through writing for publications such as Brainz Magazine, speaking, teaching, and sharing Universal Energy sessions.

Having embraced her lineage as a storyteller of souls, she unlocks the secrets hidden by your ancestral fate and deepest fears as a mirror for others to see themselves as she and the universe see them. Kelly will assist you in reawakening your true being through a path of awareness with compassion of your karmic fate with a deeper understanding of how to create your destiny. Her ability to whisper the wisdom of universal energy, her ancestors, and the animal kingdom, will leave you with an open heart and open mind to expand your intentional awareness of what is possible in your own life.

Connect with Kelly:

www.BeyondWordsNWisdom.com

www.facebook.com/kelly.l.mccarthy.9

Notes

Chapter 15

Rebel Yell: Embracing the Leader Within

Barb Pritchard

One of my catch phrases as a child was, "You're not the boss of me." What can I say? I'm a rebel at heart. (Bless my parents' hearts!)

I've been going against the grain since I entered this world. I was expected to be Jonathan David, a boy, and was supposed to be born on October 5th. But another path was laid out before me. I entered this world as Barbara on November 5th, rebel Scorpio, at your pleasure.

I've often been told I do things the difficult way. My dad and my exes all muttered expressions of frustration at my rebellious, stubborn streak. Others have painted my penchant for freedom as being a trailblazer, but it didn't dawn on me until very recently that even in rebellion comes leadership.

Don't get me wrong - I don't shirk responsibility. I come from a family where a strong work ethic and education are the recipe for success. My mom has always said, "You can do anything you put your mind to as long as you work hard for it." It didn't help that my X chromosome seemingly made that hill significantly steeper to climb.

In my days of corporate, I would work my booty off. It's just what you did. When it came to accepting roles in management, though, I would vehemently refuse. My husband and I have talked ad nauseum about how neither of us wanted to be a manager. Too much red tape and zero interest in bureaucracy. It didn't help that my facial expressions weren't conducive to brown-nosing, and never mind, the weight of responsibility for the well-being of others was a burden we just didn't want to bear. I'm way too direct and "what-you-see-is-what-you-get" to work well as a manager. At least, that's what I told myself. Teenage Barb would sneer at the idea of Manager Barb and call her a sell-out.

However, looking back, as my career progressed, there was a pattern of naturally attracting like-minded people around me at my place of employment. These groups would seemingly magnetically come together and essentially become work-family, a safe space to vent frustrations and share laughs. I would help find a silver lining in situations, leading a group of women where we lifted one another up to continue the slog through the 9-5 grind. We all felt seen, heard, and understood. No one felt alone in their struggles.

Though I never saw myself as a leader.

It wasn't until 2021 that I started to lift the veil and see myself as a... ((nervous gulp)) Leader with a Big L. It all happened naturally - and also very fast! All it took was what I call stepping into my magic, no longer muting my voice or rounding out my edges. I let go of the facade, which represented what I thought was expected of me. (Been there, done that, got the t-shirt, and burned it.)

In my case, this meant the time had come to proudly wave my Weird Flag. I felt called to embrace my intuitive side. As a brand and web designer with 20+ years in the corporate world, especially as a user-experience designer with whom all things must be tested and numbers are mission-critical, this went against everything I knew. But the call to become an Intuitive Designer was strong and not one to be ignored any longer.

Once I truly understood and embraced what it meant to answer this call, things fell into place. I discovered a new, now beloved friend who was launching an Introduction to Oracle Card course. It was as if she had a pillar of light shining onto her; I knew I needed this goodness in my life. Taking Robin Finney's course unlocked a whole new world for me. I was introduced to many like-minded, heart-centered women who easily "got it." While I thought I felt seen and heard in my previous work-family circles, it was never quite to this degree.

From there, more aligned opportunities became available to me. I was invited to join the Ladies' Power Lunch group - a group of heart-centered entrepreneurs who intentionally support one another in aligned ways. This group of women (and a few spectacular men) take the ick out of networking. It felt like family right from the jump.

I was introduced to my soul-sister and BFF, Dr.Davia Shepherd. We hit it off instantly, both recognizing there's something extraordinary about this connection we have, though we didn't fully understand it at the time. Being in Davia's world means collaboration opportunities abound. More soul-aligned women entered into my world and swept me off of my feet in a whirlwind of abundant success.

Conformity Killed the Radio Star

Far too often, we hide the best, most interesting parts of ourselves so we can "fit in." Maybe we're afraid our brand of weird will repel the wrong people. As a result, at least what I've found to be true, we end up attracting muted versions of others and opportunities as well. I see it in my client work. Muted versions of anything lack passion... and ain't nobody got time for half-hearted attempts at this thang called life.

Let's not forget that to make a ripple or a rising tide, we have to get noticed. And you can't get noticed if you don't stand out.

As I write this, I can't help but chuckle to myself, thinking of a time when I felt ready to make a ripple but not yet ready to shed a certain air of professionalism. In 2017, the previous iteration of Infinity Brand Design was called Third Eye Creative Design. My catchphrase was, "you can't get noticed if you don't stand out." But back then, I was still too scared to truly walk the walk. Both rebel and introvert, standing out and getting noticed was a scary notion, not to mention ironic. How does an introvert handle attention without having the life force sucked out? My rebellious nature made standing out a common thing, but I wasn't fully ready to stand in my truth or own my magic.

Looking back, I realize it was my inability to dive deep and embrace *all of myself* that held me back. I tried many times over the past 20+ years to build a successful business with steady work. Many times, I failed, but I never gave up. What I didn't realize until recently was that it wasn't my offer that needed changing. Not my business name. Not even my skills. I see now that I was still afraid to lean into my intuition, my woo-woo factor, and fully embrace my spirituality, thinking I would be called a charlatan, even though I've had fine art training and a degree in web design.

Answering this call to step into my magic in 2020 was the catalyst that unlocked many opportunities for me in business that I had only ever dreamed of. And embracing leadership naturally came with it. (Now, now, Teenage Barb, no need to cringe, I assure you.)

I've learned when you show up confidently, wholly you, you're magnetic. Like-minded people show up and see you. They want to understand how they, too, can feel so comfortable and confident. They want to surround themselves with like-minded folks who aren't afraid to be themselves. They want to be able to confidently and fearlessly talk about their passion. Who knew this is the epitome of leadership? I sure didn't. Whether you ask for it or not, leadership finds a way. (Who read that in Jeff Goldblum's voice?) But it doesn't have to feel heavy.

For my fellow rebels out there (I'm lookin' at you, Teenage Barb), there's a way to be seen as a leader without feeling like a sell-out. Show up unapologetically, authentically you; Leadership (with a Big L!) comes part-and-parcel.

Interestingly enough, Big L Leadership doesn't scare me. It doesn't even feel burdensome. It's quite the opposite. It feels easy because the pressure to perform doesn't exist. (Which, interestingly enough, also removes the essence of competition, making room for collaboration instead!)

How can that be so?

I believe stepping into your truth, your true essence, requires keeping your cause, and your purpose (I call this your magic) front and center. Keep your eye on the prize, so to speak. Shifting my focus on *who* and *how* I can help has removed the burden of the "gotta-get-a-new-client, bills-gotta-get-paid" frenzy. I'm just here to help. I just happen to have a particular set of skills (who read that in *Liam Neeson's* voice?) I also have certain talents that can be tapped into to utilize said help.

This shift to "how can I help" and embracing Big L Leadership has been eye-opening. As I mentioned before, it eradicates the sense of competition and instead invites collaboration. It expands beyond the scarcity mindset and invites one of abundance. After all, as heart-centered entrepreneurs, we're all here to make the world a better place. I like to say we're all here to help do-gooders do super goodness, one person at a time. Stepping into Big L Leadership is essential to making that ripple, or dare I say to create that rising tide that lifts all boats!

Collaboration Over Competition = Big L Leadership

When I was fresh out of college, I was taken for a ride by a client who saw me coming a mile away. I had no boundaries, no contract, and no real understanding of my value or worth. I designed three different brands and websites for him before getting paid a dime. Needless to say, I was ghosted and lost out on a minimum of $3500.

This led me down a path of unhealthy competition I see many jaded business owners go down: where you hold your cards so close to your chest because you're so afraid to get burned again. This paralyzing strategy is equivalent to taking one step forward and five steps backward. The energy that goes along with it only works to repel clients and leaves you feeling bitter, dejected, and desperate to do anything to pay those bills.

Looking back, I wished I had found in my youth the collaborative networking opportunities that are available now. The guidance and wisdom available in groups like Ladies' Power Lunch could have provided me the clarity to learn healthy boundaries to understand what aligned collaboration looks like.

Interestingly enough, I don't feel an ounce of competition in groups like Ladies' Power Lunch. I don't even feel the need to hold my own trade secrets close to my chest, even though there are other brand and web designers in the group. I see other service providers feel very much the same way.

How can that be so?

Here's the thing. You and your magic, when you fully step into it, are the differentiator. There is nothing anyone can do that can hold a flame to your magic. You stand out and shine. The beautiful part of it all is that you truly become magnetic to your star client. Sure, you also repel those who you're not meant for, and that's a-ok. Because who wants to work with those you're not meant to?

And those other service providers who do the same thing you

do... maybe they serve a different audience or purpose. Maybe they serve those whom you repel. Maybe you can team up together to refer one another. You'd be surprised at how quickly referral partnerships can be formed.

I invite you, my Friend, to step into your own brand of weirdness, whatever that may be to you. Go against the grain. Stand out and shine. Partner up and collaborate. Embrace that Big L Leader within. Then watch as the opportunities unfold.

Do you struggle with embracing your role in leadership?

I assure you, if you're an entrepreneur, you are a leader.

I invite you to create a space where you can dive a bit deeper into what's blocking you from owning that Big L Leadership status.

Close your eyes and envision yourself as a leader.

What emotions and thoughts come up for you?

Perhaps, like me, you've been a leader all along but haven't been able to see it because you can't see the label from inside the bottle.

What comes up for you if you were to shift your perspective to "how can I help"? Does that feel less heavy and remove the added pressure we tend to put on ourselves? Big L Leadership doesn't have to be a heavy weight to bear.

Do you struggle with embracing collaboration over competition?

What emotions and thoughts come up for you? Journal on these emotions and thoughts to see where your intuition leads you. I invite you to pull a card as this may help guide your intuition. Sometimes all we need are a few boundaries in place for a collaboration to feel aligned. Trust your intuition. It is a worthy guide!

Want to take your magic to the next level? Download the free Soul-Aligned Brand Vision Workbook. It will helps you put your magic into context by surfacing visuals that represent the essence of your magic. You can then utilize visuals similar to these and use them throughout your brand, website, social media, and launches. Think of this as a vision board for your business or next launch!

"I invite you, my Friend, to step into your own brand of weirdness, whatever that may be to you. Go against the grain. Stand out and shine. Partner up and collaborate. And embrace that Big L Leader within. Then watch as the opportunities unfold."

~Barb Pritchard

About Barb Pritchard

Barb Pritchard is a brand enchanter, website wizard, sales page sage, and book cover/launch magician for spiritual entrepreneurs. She helps soulful businesses look like the abundance they manifest, raise their vibe, and infuse their magic into their business through purposeful, empathy-focused design. Barb is a believer in the magic of marrying Spirit with strategy to create an impactful and remarkable business that attracts clients automagically.

With over 20 years of design experience with both Fortune 100/500 clients and small businesses, Barb's passion is empowering heart-centered entrepreneurs to feel more fulfilled within their business and make a bigger impact by sharing their magic and infusing it into every client interaction in their business.

When she's not designing, Barb can be found snuggling with her mini-panthers, nerding out with her husband playing video games or Dungeons and Dragons, or planning their next excursion to Europe to experience the culture, the food, and the history.

Connect with Barb:

www.InfinityBrand.Design

www.facebook.com/InfinityBrandDesign

www.instagram.com/infinitybranddesign

www.linkedin.com/in/barbpritchard

Free Soul-Aligned Brand Vision Workbook:

www.soul-alignedbrand.com

Notes

Chapter 16

Heterarchy - An Invitation to Lead in a New Way

Dr. Davia Shepherd

Hi! I'm Dr. Davia, and I host the Ladies' Power Lunch Group, the amazing group of women responsible for publishing this series of transformational anthologies. My official title in our organization is CHO: Chief Happiness Officer. Already, from my title, you can probably tell that as the happiness officer, I'm serious when I talk about us having a new paradigm of leadership! You can tell that I'm serious when I suggest that instead of considering leadership in terms of hierarchy, we consider a new way to get things done: HETERARCHY.

I met and fell in love with the word heterarchy. In my defense, I'm a word nerd. I mean, if you were a word nerd, I think you would fall in love with HETERARCHY too. I've been called many things; my favorite is being called the queen of collaboration. As a word, HETERARCHY seems to embody the spirit of collaboration and cooperation that I would love to see as I navigate every area of my life, including my business relationships. Usually, the theme/spirit of our anthologies, summits, or retreats comes to me in meditation or quiet contemplation. When I quiet my mind and listen, a strange thing happens: thoughts come in that appear not to be coming from me directly and, more often than not, have significance beyond what I could imagine.

This time around, Divine Beloved, sassy broad that she is, spoke to me through the voice of a woman that I am honored to call a friend. Linda Albright and I were chatting away, and in the course of our deep, meaningful conversation, Heterarchy was something she mentioned. Word nerd that I am, I raced to the dictionary and was greeted by all the great definitions, from math to psychology, to social sciences, to coding, to human resources. I, dear friend, was in word nerd nirvana.

Based on my research into this newer word added to my lexicon, I developed my own definition. I make up words all the time in conversation; why not make up definitions as well? Back when I did language and linguistics 101 in college, I'll never forget what my professor said: "language is dynamic." Those were the first words she ever said to us and words that I will remember forever. What that means for me, for you, and for all of us is that we have an opportunity right here and now to rewrite the definition of leadership to include the way we lead and the way we want leadership to support future generations.

So here's my definition of HETERARCHY: The new paradigm for leadership. This form of leadership provides each and every person with authority, sovereignty, and autonomy. Each individual assumes responsibility, depending on the circumstances of her or his area of expertise. We are all connected to each other, and we all lean in and support each other as needed. AKA: collaborative leadership, source-led leadership; the LPL way!

Each of us, as teachers, healers, authors, coaches, speakers, and professionals in all backgrounds who can hold space so that others can be the best version of themselves and tap into the highest expression of their innate gifts and talents, fit into the definition of LEADERS, in this Heterarchy. And so, dear one, listen to me as I say this in Oprah's voice: you are a leader, and you are a leader! EVERYBODY IS A LEADER!!!!

When Elizabeth Hill, Barb Prichard, and I got together and started planning this anthology and summit, with Coleen

Brunetti's help, we arrived at the title "Ignite Your Leadership," which I love so much. Often when we think of leadership, we think of our grandfather's idea of leadership: top-down, hierarchical leadership when there is one person at the top, usually a guy! In this scenario, even if the guy at the top is benevolent, we are all subject to his whims. But the times, they are a-changing. Can you feel it? Can you sense that the shift in the paradigm of leadership is happening, that it's happening now, and that this is not a drill y'all? Can you feel the energy of this?

If you are into quotes at all and you look up leadership quotes on any of the plethora of social media sites out there, you will sense this shift that I am talking about. One of my favorite quotes about leadership that I have been seeing a lot of recently is by John Quincy Adams:

"If your actions inspire others to dream more, learn more, do more and become more, you are a leader."

You are a leader, YES, YOU!

Me, at my first Leaders Anonymous meeting: *My name is Davia Hyacinth Shepherd, and I'm a leader!*

Everyone in unison: *Hi, Davia!*

I've been reluctant to call myself a leader. I know many of you will identify with how I have felt over the years. Just like you, I've been happily doing the work I do. Just like you, I have actually truly been leading in my own quiet behind-the-scenes way. And just like you, I have shied away from accepting the official title. Well, guess what? I'm a born leader, and you are too!

I should have known better. It's in my name, for heaven's sake. Davia means beloved, and a shepherd is another term for guide. Am I right? Well, Hyacinth is just a pretty purple flower, so my name actually means beloved pretty flower guide. Sounds great; I'll take it!

I should have been clued in by my name but as often happens when things are right in front of our eyes, I didn't see the signs! I never set out to call myself any kind of leader. I was taught to be humble. Many of us learn to be self-deprecating very early in life. Ascribing the term leader to myself seemed too pompous, too grandiose for me. And that was because I was thinking of leadership in the way that the old paradigm described. Well, as I said, it was right in front of me. It was right there in my name.

"Leadership is about making others better as a result of your presence... and that impact lasting in your absence." -Unknown

I love this quote. If that's what the new paradigm of leadership is all about, then golly-George, sign me up! I want to support others in any way I can, I want my presence in others' lives to have a positive impact; I want people to be positively influenced even after our interaction has ended! Does that sound like what you want out of your interactions as well? If you do, my dear buttercup, then you are a leader! Pure and simple.

I started out thinking that I wanted to be a pharmacologist. Most of us have dreams that somehow we would have a contribution that would influence the greater good, and that was mine. My plan was to work on a team that makes a drug that helps people feel better. Even back then, in my teens, when this dream was born, I knew that I wanted to work in a way that would influence many people's lives. The vehicle for making this happen was Pharma, and I worked in that field happily as a team member for many years.

My definition of the new paradigm of Leadership includes being able to hold space so that others can be the best version of themselves and tap into the highest expression of their innate gifts and talents. Pretty much just BE a safe space. That I can do, that we all in this space can do. That's how I believe was born, my journey into accepting myself as the "leader."

Back in my corporate life, I would find that I would often be called on to "lead" committees and "lead" initiatives and eventually was invited to a training/coaching role. That was my favorite; that was what it seemed I excelled at. That role invited me to do a lot of speaking, teaching, and presenting, and I realized that I had a gift for breaking down somewhat complicated science into very easy-to-understand terms. I also drew on my school experience, where I'd often tutor or coach other students. I'd find that even as I was teaching it, I was learning it more solidly, and that may have contributed to getting good grades.

So there I was, working in what I considered a quasi-leadership role when I moved away from corporate and started working in private holistic practice. I still didn't consider my position in corporate truly as leadership because it was more leading from beside, linking arms and being supportive, holding space, and coaching; not the "my way or the highway" kind of leadership I had become accustomed to.

"A sign of a good leader is not how many followers you have but how many leaders you create." ~Mahatma Gandhi

Ignite your leadership

Getting called on to be in charge of stuff seems to happen to me all the time, just routinely. People like to assign tasks to people who will get stuff done. I've been a chronic over-doer in my life, and so it is truly no wonder. I would be called upon to be the "leader" of committees or teams, or groups all through the years all my life.

Which is hilarious because I can only deal with being in

company for a short time, then I go into introvert mode. The life and times of an ambivert! It just goes to show that your personality type doesn't dictate your being a leader. The only thing that determines that is if you choose it if you accept the calling and ignite your leadership.

Here's the true short story version of what happened in my case. Many of our members have heard this one before, so if you know it, sing along. If you are hearing it for the first time, learn it well, because there will be a test! ;)

I left corporate and started in private practice at a time when getting new patients was difficult. I met some amazing women networking at the local chamber of commerce, and we decided to have lunch which turned out to be amazing. We decided that we needed to do this every month, and Ladies' Power Lunch™ was born. We have gone from six women on that first day to an international group through the power of women wanting to support each other. That's how I got the call I could not ignore. I was invited by life to be the beacon for beacons, to answer the call, and to ignite my leadership in a completely different way from my initial intention, which was to be a pharmacologist, and it happened quite unexpectedly.

In this anthology, Ignite your Leadership, you have encountered inspiring stories from LEADERS just like you who have embraced this new paradigm. They love the idea that as they light up to the idea that they are indeed leaders and that we lead now in this way where we are all linking arms and supporting each other, that this helps the people, we are meant to work with light up more fully, and then they light up their people and on and on it goes until the world vibrates at that high level we all desire.

You have read stories from some of our authors who ignited their leadership as they encountered some hardships or tough times. These stories are so inspirational and really show us our resilient nature and that often, even out of the greatest perceived adversity can come learning.

Some stories share the new idea of leadership and how our authors are leading in their organizations, their communities, and their businesses with compassion, strength, empathy, and collaboration. Truly sharing examples that we can apply to our own lives and businesses.

Then there are the stories to which I relate so well; stories from those of us who have never ever considered the idea of leadership, never considered the leadership role for ourselves, and who lead by example, lead through collaboration and lead even against all odds.

Meditation

Close your eyes and take a deep breath in; hold that breath and exhale. Do that again 2-3 times, grounding yourself and your energy.

Now settle into your breathing and imagine that you are breathing in pure positive energy of the universe and exhaling your divine light of love and support going out into the world.

Imagine that as you breathe out your beautiful light, it is touching all the beautiful souls in the world that you are meant to work with. These are the amazing people that may, at this moment, be losing sleep at night because they so very much need the work that you do.

Imagine them taking in your light and they themselves lighting up. Keep breathing and imagine that as they light up that the lives that they are meant to touch light up as well. Imagine a ripple effect of people lighting up all over the world until the world is filled with beautiful light from your heart.

Now breathe in that beautiful light that has made its way around the planet and imagine the planet lighting up the universe.

Questions:

1. What came up for you as you imagined this beautiful scenario?

2. What ideas does this bring up for you related to leadership?

3. In what ways do you think you can employ HETERARCHY in your life and your business?

About Davia H. Shepherd

Dr. Davia Shepherd wears a lot of hats. She is a mom, a sister, a daughter, and a wife. She helps her my patients feel better every day. Davia is a bestselling author and a professional speaker and she hoss and coordinates our women's collaboration collective Ladies Power Lunch - LPL.

The thing that she is most passionate about, the one thing that gets her out of the bed in the mornings and into the office on a Monday, is the opportunity to support women in business to live their optimal lives: to grow their visibility, reach, impact and their income.

Davia is an amplifier. She has almost two decades of experience (in the corporate world as well as running her own community practice) with her innate ability to translate the energetic signature of the best version of you, into words. That big dream that you didn't even know you had, for both your business and your life? She not only can translate that for you, but also makes it bigger, using it to develop a solid plan for increased visibility, reach, and success. The result is that you shine your light at its most brilliant; that you stop being the world's best-kept secret. Your optimal clients, the ones that are losing sleep at night because they need you, the ones who light up when you work together, are then able to find you with ease and grace; and you can live your passion, be seen, be heard, and be visible.

Connect with Davia:
www.growsmarternotharder.com

Grow Smarter:
Source-Led Visibility
for Your Business

You can grow your business in challenging times with ease and flow. You can be seen, be heard, and be visible. Download Dr. Davia's book **Grow Smarter- Collaboration Secrets to Transform Your Income and Impact** for free with Amazon Kindle Unlimited. As a bonus, get the Grow Smarter course, a step by step guide for applying Grow Smarter principles to your business, for **free**:

www.growsmarternotharder.com/course

Do you want to know more about the **LPL Grow Smarter method** for getting you and your business seen, heard, and visible, in an aligned way and with ease and flow? Go to:

www.growsmarternotharder.com

GREEN HEART
LIVING
— PRESS —

Green Heart Living Press publishes inspirational books and stories of transformation, making the world a more loving and peaceful place, one book at a time.

Whether you have an idea for an inspirational book and want support through the writing process – or your book is already written and you are looking for a publishing path – Green Heart Living can help you get your book out into the world.

You can meet Green Heart authors on the Green Heart Living YouTube channel and the Green Heart Living Podcast.

www.GreenHeartLiving.com